GAINESBORO, TENNESSEE
LOGAN, NEW MEXICO

Southeast
by Southwest

Village Scenes Century to Century

J. L. WALKER

WalkAbout Press   Brentwood, Tennessee

Published by WalkAbout Press
P. O. Box 2903
Brentwood, Tennessee 37024
jlwwalker1@gmail.com

Printed in the United States of America

ISBN 978-0-615-55443-3

Acknowledgments

The essays in *Southeast by Southwest: Village Scenes Century to Century* have been a work in progress for more years than I want to count. Over the years I've had help from many writers and from others interested in the stories the essays tell.

Thanks to the various members of the writing group that meets two Saturdays a month at the Williamson County Library in Franklin, Tennessee, but thanks especially to Sally Rodes Lee and Louise Colln, who through the years have listened to most of these essays, sometimes more than once. Their comments always helped me see where more—and sometimes less—was needed.

Thanks also to the writing group that came together as part of the Osher Lifelong Learning Institute at Vanderbilt University and to the group's guide and mentor Victor Judge. In the two-year course he called The Writing Life, he responded to each writer's work with a commitment that enlarged our understanding of what it means to actually have a writing life.

Writing the essay about J. H. and Joe Shollenbarger would have been so much more difficult without the help of

Kenneth Shollenbarger, of Amarillo, Texas, son of Joe Shollenbarger, whom I interviewed not long before his death in 2000. Kenneth provided copies of family photos, photos of Logan landmarks, and newspaper articles about the village. Seeing photos taken over a century ago gave me an insight into the family and the times that I otherwise could not have had. Thanks also to his daughter Helen Eller, who provided digitized photos.

Special thanks to Jane Russ of Nashville, who gave freely of her time and knowledge to edit copy. Thanks to Arelene Wright of Logan who provided me with important photos and for letting me make a copy of a rare postcard of the auto and railroad bridges at Logan. She also brought together a group of Logan residents who, in making a homesteaders map which appears in "Village Merchant," helped preserve some of Logan's history.

Many thanks to Eldon Walker of Nashville. His knowledge of the Logan community was especially helpful in working through the Shollenbarger and the McFarland material. His careful reading of all the essays, sometimes more than once, helped give them their final form.

Finally, thanks to Dolores Penrod of Portales, New Mexico, for her reminder through the years that it is "steady effort, steady effort" that turns a plan into reality.

J. L. Walker
Nashville, Tennessee
September, 2011

Introduction

A United States representative elected in 2010 from a place in rural Tennessee called Frog Jump, so small it's not found on a map, was recently reported to have said that he wished more Americans held the values that the citizens of Frog Jump hold.

This is a contemporary expression of an old American ideal expressed most memorably by Thomas Jefferson. Jefferson believed rural life produced citizens uncorrupted by subservience, venality, and an excess of ambition. It is rural life, he wrote, that nurtures "happiness and permanence of government."

A century later Walt Whitman took up the theme and described residents of what he called inland America. They act with freedom, he said; they're not followers, they're never obedient. They "look carelessly in the faces of presidents and governors, as to say, Who are you?"

Jefferson may have suspected that his ideal rural America was not the America of the future, and perhaps that's what led him to defend it so strongly. In his *Notes on the State of Virginia*, he wrote, "The mobs of great cities add just so much to the support of pure government, as sores do to the strength of the human body, " but his objections to cities could not change history. From the 19th century onward, fewer and fewer Americans have called rural America home. The 2010 U.S. census found that barely sixteen percent of Americans, the fewest ever, are part of a rural community.

Still, the Jeffersonian vision of America holds its place in people's hearts and imaginations. Rural life is imagined as simpler, purer, less hectic, more family centered, more connected to nature and its sustaining beauty. It is the family farm, Sergeant York, Lake Woebegon, the home of the upright and God-fearing.

Southeast by Southwest: Village Scenes Century to Century is a collection of essays about two rural American villages. Gainesboro is part of middle Tennessee's Upper Cumberland region. Logan in eastern New Mexico is part of the Llano Estacado, an area that some 150 years ago the Spanish called the Comancheria, for it was home only to the Comanches.

Gainesboro lies twenty miles south of the Kentucky border and twenty miles north of U. S. Interstate 40, the highway that takes travelers and eighteen-wheelers from the east coast to the Pacific. Settled near the beginning of the nineteenth century, the town is nestled among Tennessee hills where the Cumberland River turns westward before looping its way south down to Nashville.

Straight west of Gainesboro on I-40, past Nashville, over the Mississippi River at Memphis, past Little Rock, Ft. Smith, Oklahoma City, through Amarillo in the Texas Panhandle, just across the New Mexico line and twenty miles north of I-40 is Logan, settled at the beginning of the 20th century.

Both towns exist as part of Americans' westward journey, and both could become permanent settlements only after the resistance of the native tribes had been eliminated. Most Tennesseans arrived by wagon via Daniel Boone's famed Wilderness Road—or, as one observer noted, any way they could. A hundred years later Logan's settlers arrived by wagon or by railroad—if by railroad, often with all their belongings, including livestock, in a box car.

I first became aware of Gainesboro in 2006. On a slow afternoon as I was driving through Jackson County toward a house I'd bought on Turkey Town Road in Clay County, I decided to take a look at the town's square and its courthouse, whose cupola I could just glimpse from Highway 56. I didn't know that afternoon that I would want to know more about Gainesboro, or that I would find books written about Tennessee's Upper Cumberland, its geology, history, and people, or that I would find people there willing to talk with me. I found Therold Richardson, then eighty-four, who grew up in the area and talked about his life and the changes he lived with and through. On Tuesday nights local musicians came together in his real estate and auction office on the square for an evening of bluegrass, gospel, and country music. As the prime mover of the Little Opry in Gainesboro, he brought together each month area musicians and a large, enthusiastic audience.

Some while after my look at the town square, I walked

up to the third floor of the courthouse and found the Jackson County Archives and Glenn Jones. I learned that his life took a new direction when he discovered Jackson County's court documents in disarray in the courthouse basement. He set out to bring order to the documents and learned how difficult such an effort can be. As an extension of an archival project, he developed the Upper Cumberland Veterans Hall and went on to create the Putnam County Archives and Veterans Hall in Cookeville, twenty miles east of Gainesboro.

I believe villages especially need individuals who practice what I call artful living. This takes a variety of forms, but for these essays I mean those people who take on a project that allows them to simultaneously create and preserve. As rural populations decline and young people leave to find jobs elsewhere, villages are at risk of losing their past, and to save it something new has to be created. Glenn Jones helped create the Jackson County Archives and created the Upper Cumberland Veterans Hall. I follow these creations in a group of essays I call "Glenn Jones: It Will Happen."

Over several years I attended Gainesboro's annual Poke Sallet Festival, its Memorial Day observance, and the Little Opry. I visited with residents and attended various meetings of community groups, including a contentious meeting of the Public Records Commission. I attended a planning meeting called to consider the restoration of an abandoned school building. The planning meeting drew a big crowd, and restoration of the school became an ongoing project.

I also interviewed Pamela Walton, the reporter who covered the Sheriff Bean sexual harassment scandal for the Jackson County *Sentinel,* a weekly with more than a century of publishing history. The scandal lit up the *Sentinel* and online chat rooms for many a month.

Although I quote from various sources in the essays, I provide formal footnotes only for the brief historical overview found in "Steamboat Prosperity and Civil War Misery."

The Gainesboro essays make up the first section of the book. The Logan essays comprise the second part. I was born in Tucumcari, twenty miles south of Logan. I started the first grade in the Logan School under the tutelage of Mrs. Claunch, and walked across the stage in the school gym twelve years later to receive my diploma.

Because I grew up there and knew the people, the Logan pieces can be best described as personal essays. Although the essay about the Shollenbargers, "Village Merchant," derives from an interview I did with Joe Shollenbarger in 1999, in many ways it provides my own view of events. This is also true of "A Demonstration to the Authorities."

Although some of the essays in this book contain historical information, history is not their primary focus. Moreover, they are not meant as an expression of how life in rural communities is somehow superior to life elsewhere in the nation. Instead, through interviews and essays about people and their projects, their celebrations, conflicts, successes, scandals, and tragedy, I hope to give readers a picture of—and a sense of—a time and a place.

Southeast

Notice how everyone has just arrived here from a journey.
        Rumi 1207-1273

Gainesboro's Square

One of the lucky ones—and it was blind luck—I sold my California condo not long before the Great Recession ravaged home prices. However, like millions of Americans committed to believing in real estate anywhere, when I moved to Tennessee I thought it made perfect sense to put some of my extra cash toward a cabin in the hills, at, of course, an inflated price.

I've never regretted the purchase—except when the propane tank needs refilling— for it led me into a

Cupola of Jackson County courthouse

world I would never otherwise have sought out. In the spring of 2006 on the way from Nashville to the cabin I stopped for a red light in Gainesboro. Usually my interest was centered on the cliffs of layered limestone along the highway, but that day I looked to my left and for the first time I paid attention to the black lettering on a big white wooden sign on the other side of the traffic light. It said Gainesboro was a town on the National Register of Historic Places.

Now, I'm of those people who likes being on the road, looking out my car window at places I've never seen before, up early when the day and the world feels new, pulling into a Sonic when it's 95 degrees in the shade, joining the night travelers as clouds drift across the moon.

However, friends point out to me that there's more to traveling than just driving. Real travelers, they say, consult guidebooks, make plans, call ahead, investigate tourist attractions, roam museums and historic houses. So, when I saw that Gainesboro merited a spot on the National Register of Historic Places, I thought, well, here might be something like a drive-through museum. I looked in the direction an arrow pointed. I could see the upper part of a large building topped by a cupola with a clock, which I figured was a county courthouse.

When the light turned green, I turned left and drove up the hill.

I didn't know exactly what I'd find at the top of the hill, but I wasn't surprised at what was—and wasn't—there. In my travels I've seen many town squares like Gainesboro's, not just the three-story yellow-brick county courthouse surrounded by red brick store fronts, but town squares that are no longer the center of a rural community. Driving east out of California into the southwest, midwest and south, travelers who veer off the freeway find towns like Gainesboro. What they were in the past is evident, what the future holds unclear.

I saw I was on Hull Street; the name almost certainly referred to Cordell Hull, for the street was just one of many places in the area I'd seen honoring Hull, probably the most famous man ever born in the Upper Cumberland. I knew a little about him—that he was Franklin's Roosevelt's Secretary of State (and the nation's longest serving Secretary of State) and that he won the Nobel Peace Prize in 1945 for his part in the establishment of the United Nations. In photographs he looked like a saint, but was known to have an amazing store of profanity. I also knew that he was instrumental in passing the U.S. federal income tax and inheritance tax laws of 1916, apparently laws some Tennesseans then and now look upon with serious disfavor.

I circled Gainesboro's square and parked in front of Trotty's Treasures, a store on the north side of the square. In his book *The Tipping Point* Malcolm Gladwell theorizes that a time comes in a chain of events when what *could* happen *will* happen. One of his examples is of a neighborhood that faces the possibility of decline but clings to respectability. Then, broken windows in an empty building go too long unrepaired; possibility turns into probability as decay sets in.

GAINESBORO'S SQUARE THAT AFTERNOON in 2006 was not full of broken windows, but it was not a busy place. Trotty's Treasures was closed, as was Pappy's next to it. Through Pappy's plate glass window I could see two hardback books stood up for display: *The Uncivil War: Irregular Warfare in the*

Upper South 1861-65 and *Myths of the Cherokee*. I was interested and walked into the shop a couple of doors down to ask about Pappy. A woman there continued energetically dusting furniture as she narrowed her eyes, shook her head, and said, "I don't know a thing about that." She turned out to be the proprietor of the Picket Fence—she was expanding her business to include the shop next to Pappy's. The furniture she was arranging included a small chest of drawers in the popular, and in this case very authentic looking, "cracked white" style. The price tag said $350, which I thought indicated some level of prosperity among shoppers.

When I stepped back out on the sidewalk I saw a sign that took up most of the wall of a brick building across the street—W. T. Reed Groceries in big yellow letters on a deep green background above the famous Coca-Cola signature in white on a red background. To the left an advertisement for Wild Goose Flour took up another part of the brick wall. I walked a little way out into Hull Street to look at the roof of the building and saw two large ornamental standing lions guarding each end, their two cubs lying in the center. I suspected the lions had stood as the building's guardians for many a year, but W. T. Reed Groceries was now the Shady Rose Gift Shop.

I walked past the courthouse to the other side of the square, which was Gore Street, another famous Tennessee name. I wondered if Gainesboro and Jackson County had voted for Al Gore in 2000. I knew that the state of Tennessee could not longer be counted on to vote Democratic.

A store anchoring the southeast corner had a big hand-lettered sign in its window that just said "Junk" and a smaller sign in the window that said the junk was on sale. Around the corner and down the street a barber shop sported an old-time red, white, and blue striped barber shop sign. Close by was the office of the Jackson County *Sentinel*, and farther down the Jackson County Historical Society (also closed that afternoon) occupied a narrow white wooden building. Opposite the museum was a substantial Methodist Church with stained glass windows.

Across the street from the junk store large flowing letters painted on the red brick front above two large plate glass windows announced Elaine's Fashions. I was curious about Elaine's, remembering the lovely town square women's speciality shops of my youth. However, the big rooms were filled with used clothing and shoes on help-yourself racks.

There were two cafes on the square, Faye's on the west side and the City Cafe on the east side. Faye's sign said it was open from 4:00 A.M. to 1:00 P.M, which seemed odd hours to me. As it was almost two o'clock, I went for coffee at the City Cafe. Decorated in bright yellow, it felt cheery and the waitress called me Honey. A sign on the wall at the back of each booth announced grilled hamburgers would be coming soon, so someone at the City Cafe cared enough about its customers to offer healthful hamburgers.

A few doors down from the cafe a small, grubby black and white sign over double doors invited passersby down a steep set of stairs to the Family Pool Room. An adjacent sign

5

forbade loitering, as if Mom and Dad and the kids might hang around on the sidewalk before going downstairs for a game of pool. I thought, someday I'll walk down those stairs.

I suspected that the Family Pool Room had held its place on the square for many a year, but two other businesses indicated a fashionably youthful clientele. One, a tanning salon, had a shop on Hull Street just down from the square. I've observed it's a rare community in Tennessee that's without a tanning salon. The other, the Relaxing Touch on Gore Street, offered massages, though that afternoon the masseuse was out. What, I wondered, had convinced someone that there was a market for massages in Gainesboro?

A furniture store, a gift shop, an automotive store, dental, real estate and attorney offices seemed to be going concerns. Two corner drug stores still had soda fountains, but neither offered old time treats. One included a gift shop and the other specialized in hospital and nursing home equipment. I'd heard that drug stores can stay in business on a town square because the cost of drugs—Medicare prescriptions, for example—varies little from pharmacy to pharmacy.

The east side of the three-story yellow brick courthouse held two items of historical interest. One, a modern looking bust in steel, portrayed Andrew Jackson at his most Old

Hickorish—full hair, commanding eyes set in a sharp-angled face above military epaulets. Its plaque read "Dedicated to the memory of Alice Hawkens Whilson of Dodson's Branch by her grandson Sam T. Barnes, the sculptor AD 2001." The other was a large marble slab engraved with the names of Jackson County men who served in WWI, WWII, Korea and Vietnam. Those who served in WWII make up by far most of the names—fifty from this rural county in Tennessee—a reminder of how vast that war was and how much it required from the nation to win it.

On the other side of the courthouse a historical marker commemorated the discovery in 1796 of the native ornamental yellowwood tree (*cladrastis tulea*). The plaque says French botanist Andre Michaux discovered the tree during his stay at Fort Blount, a late eighteenth century military outpost on the Cumberland River. The yellowwood was designated Tennessee's Bicentennial Tree in 1992.

The building itself had an entrance on all four sides, but the west door was the most elaborate, with a porch and columns and a decorative center section with the year 1927 inscribed near the top of the building. Centered above the door and above the third story bank of windows was a decorative frieze—a center piece balanced on each side by a drapery scroll—in what I later learned historians call the neoclassical revival style. A large urn decorated each corner of the building. The round clock in the cupola had black numbers in a classical script. The hands said it was 7:45.

Taped to the door of the entrance were two flyers, one

inviting the community to a benefit for a local family struck by illness, the other an announcement of a meeting to discuss the local drug problem. Inside the first floor with its high ceiling were county offices, and a sign beside a narrow stair pointed the way to a courtroom.

On leaving I found in a hallway a series of framed documents identified as "Foundations of American Law and Government." The first document hung on the wall was the Mayflower Compact, next the Declaration of Independence, then the Ten Commandments, the Magna Carta, the Star Spangled Banner, The National Motto "In God We Trust" (passed by the U. S. Congress in 1956), the Preamble to the Tennessee Constitution, and The Bill of Rights. The inclusion of the Mayflower Compact, the Magna Carta, the Ten Commandments, and the national motto made a clear statement of Bible Belt values.

Back in my car I explored some of the blocks beyond the square. Historical information signs said the square and a block off each side of it made up the historical district.

Through the summer and fall I walked the square from time to time. In July and August the paved streets, the three-story yellow brick courthouse, and the dark brick store fronts increased the stifling heat. Then, none too soon, in autumn the square regained its spirits. More cars, pots of yellow chrysanthemums in the flower boxes on the corners, business windows with a scrawled message on a big sheet of butcher paper urging the high school football team on to victory.

In October next to the Relaxing Touch on Gore Street I found the recently opened Jackson County Democratic Headquarters ready for the 2006 elections. There I talked with life-long Democrat Ben Hix, who had served as a County Democratic Chairman but that fall was donating time to help keep the Headquarters open. Jackson County votes Democratic, said Hix, whose family came to the Upper Cumberland in 1799 and whose Hix listing is one of forty-six in the Gainesboro phone book. He pointed out that in terms of the percentage of citizens voting Democratic, Jackson County is number one in Tennessee. * "This is not because we are so popular," he stressed, "but because we work hard at it." He would have liked to see Democrats seeking state or national office make Gainesboro a campaign stop just to say thanks, but, he said, they don't. Gov. Bredesen promised to come but hadn't. "There's all this big talk," Hix said, "about somebody who gives $10,000—or more—but what does that say? What about the people? I'd never give that much money, even if I had it."

I had a massage at the Relaxing Touch. The people were friendly and talkative, and I was sorry when later I saw that their sign on the glass door was gone. I kept checking Pappy's window. *The Uncivil War: Irregular Warfare in the Upper South 1861-65* and *Myths of the Cherokee* kept their same prominent place on the wooden book shelf, but I never found Pappy's open.

---

*Jackson County gave Barack Obama thirty-nine more votes (2,224) than it gave John McCain (2,185). Next closest was Ralph Nader with 44 votes and Bob Barr (Libertarian) with 16. Total votes cast was 4,501. It was one of six Tennessee counties to go Democratic in 2008.

A Sliver of Time on the Highland Rim

Just north of Gainesboro where Roaring River flows into the Cumberland, gray limestone cliffs stand a hundred feet high. The Cumberland and the cliffs exposed by the river carving its way through the rock over millennia make for a scenic drive north from Gainesboro to Celina, twenty miles away.

The Cumberland River outside Gainesboro in October

It's true that the Cumberland River is not one of those storied rivers inseparable from the people who live near its shores, like the Ganges and the Hindus, the Thames and Londoners, or the Mississippi and Mark Twain. It's not famed for commerce or for steamboats that once drew revelers and gamblers. Yet there is about it an aura of history, a mystique, if you will. In early spring as the river rises, a few adventurers take up with their inner Huck Finn in the brief days before summer muscles in. Little waterfalls flow over the grey cliffs, some beginning high up and out of sight, some breaking right out of the rock itself. Atop the cliffs, earth energy rises toward a blue sky, and the year's supply of leaves unfurls.

The autumn lingers through October and most of November. After Thanksgiving the sky is mostly grey and so is the diminished river. Topped by leafless trees the grey cliffs take on a bleak, elemental appearance. Another year draws to a close.

It has been only a short while—a sliver of time— since humans have been around to mark the end of one year and the start of another. The Earth is old, many eons older than humanity and the Cumberland. Some people describe the Earth's age, about four and a half billion years, as barely comprehensible to the human mind. It's more accurate to say that four and a half billion years is totally incomprehensible to the human mind, as is 250 million, or a million, for that matter. For most of the hundreds of millions of years the Earth has seen sunrise and sunset, little is known. Intense heat, belching volcanos, lava, then, some believe, a period so cold the Earth made its annual swing around the sun as a giant snowball.

Of that four and a half billion years, it is in rocks formed over the last billion that geologists find a comprehensive history—what you might call intimations of Earth time. In Tennessee, the history the rocks tell is extensive, with "only a few major gaps in the record of events in that great length of time," writes Robert A. Miller in his *The Geologic History of Tennessee*.

To touch some billion-year-old stuff, a traveler can go

due east from Gainesboro to the Tennessee-North Carolina border in Carter County. That border area is the only place in Tennessee where rocks formed from lava, or from compacted volcanic ash and dust, or from extreme variations in temperature and chemical environment lie on the surface. Geologists call rock of this kind the basement complex. Thousands of feet deep, it's mostly everywhere buried under a layer of sedimentary rock that is itself as much as two and a half miles deep. And, this miles-deep layer, says Dr. Michael Harrison, head of the Geology Department at Tennessee Technological University in Cookeville, represents only one percent of the volume of the earth's surface — "It's like the layering of a piece of paper on a basketball."

So, it turns out that the visible cliffs just outside Gainesboro and all over middle Tennessee represent just the top of sedimentary layers that accumulated when water from ancient oceans advanced over North America, then receded, time and again.

How there came to be enough water to fill these oceans is not a totally settled issue, but it's certain the earth had to cool down before water could accumulate. Initially, gases released when volcanos erupted may have produced the steam which became clouds as the earth's surface, called the crust, cooled. Rain fell for thousands and thousands and thousands of years, but even that much rain doesn't account for all the water that covers three fourths of the earth's surface. Much of it, says Dr. Harrison, came from ice comets holding hundreds of thousands of gallons of water colliding with the earth. There was much crashing and banging about in those billions of years when planetary debris zoomed through outer space at some 90,000 mph and our solar system had yet to settle down.

Some 500 million years ago, there was, says John McPhee in his book *In Suspect Terrain,* more ocean over North America than at anytime since. The sea had advanced over the continent at an average rate of ten miles a year, and middle Tennessee, along with most of what is now the United States, was underwater.

If you had paddled east out of Gainesboro you would have found yourself at the deep ocean's edge just the other side of the North Carolina border. There was no Mexico or Central America. If you had headed west, you might have waded some of the way on white beaches, but you wouldn't have found land much above water until you reached the Texas Panhandle. Most of New Mexico was above water, but at the Arizona border, the ocean claimed everything. A ridge of land extended out of New Mexico to the north, widening out into a huge land mass in Canada. Had you followed the ridge as far as Kearney, Nebraska, you would have found "a blistering-hot equatorial beach," writes McPhee. Turning west and past Laramie, Wyoming, "you would have come to a west-facing beach, and after it, tidal mudflats all the way to Utah. The waters of the shelf would now begin to deepen. A hundred miles into Nevada was the continental slope and beyond it the blue ocean."

Water reigned and so did silence. Invertebrate animal life flourished in the shallow seas. Shelled creatures developed, died and drifted down to the sea floor. In Tennessee, layers of limestone and of shale, sandstone, dolomite, and chert hold multitudes of fossils preserved in periods of advancing water.

Much of the sediment that these years produced lies beneath the Earth's surface all over the state. It is exposed in only three places in Tennessee, one of them five miles south of Gainesboro at Flynn's Creek. There some 360 million years ago a comet or a meteor crashed to earth, digging out a crater almost two miles in diameter. (The largest crater with a diameter of eight miles is at Wells Creek on the boundary of Houston and Stewart Counties in the southern area of middle Tennessee.) Although a shallow sea covered middle Tennessee at the time, in his *Geologic History of Tennessee* Robert Miller says the impact at Flynn's Creek "intensely deformed" rock that began as sediment and shells millions of years previously, and some rock landed a thousand feet above its normal place in the earth.

The crater is not readily visible, for it has been filled with eroded matter, principally what geologists call Chattanooga Shale. This rock came from a black mud made up of rotted organic matter deposited by a sea that covered much of the east-central United States in the same period the crater crashed to the earth. Luckily, nothing with a nose was there. The decomposed organic matter gave off hydrogen sulfide, meaning hundreds of thousands of square miles smelled like rotten eggs.

Where the Cumberland River and Roaring River converge is part of an area geologists call the Highland Rim. Its two parts, eastern and western, enclose the Central Basin, a low elliptical shaped area in the center of the state. The Highland Rim resulted from a bulge in middle Tennessee produced by continents colliding on North America's eastern coast. The bulge produced by the buckling is called the Nashville Dome. Then, over millennia the "dome" eroded away, leaving the basin and its rim. The Highland Rim is very old, older, in fact, than the Cumberland Plateau and the Appalachians to the east, and they are some of the oldest mountains on earth.

The notion of continents crashing into one another seems highly unlikely, which is probably the reason why most geologists rejected for more than half a century the theory of plate tectonics, first advanced in the early 1900s. What reasonable person could believe that once all the continents and islands were one big continent clustered around the south pole; then the big continent broke into parts, and in their ancient and in their current forms, the parts float on the earth's crust like massive jagged-edged cookies moved by a convection oven deep underground?

Dr. Harrison defines science as "basically defining the probability of something." Acceptance of plate tectonics grew among geologists because the theory accounts for the existence of mountains. Why are mountains where they are? Why are some massive and craggy like the Rockies and the Himalayas and some rounded and motherly like the Appalachians?

Plate theory says that when the continents first split

from their South Pole home, an ancient ocean geologists call Iapetus (father of Atlas/Atlantic) opened. Then it closed, as over 250 million years ancient North America/Europe and South America/Africa collided. McPhee writes: "Moving toward each other, the great land masses on either side [of Iapetus] buckled and downwarped the continental shelves and then came together in a crash no less brutal than slow — a continent-to-continent collision . . . which has reached its old age as the Appalachian Mountains."

There were actually three mountain building events, called orogenies, but the really big crash that produced the Appalachians we know now came last, beginning about 320 million years ago and concluding forty million years later. Parts of the "suture" — where the continents collided — can be seen near Brevard, North Carolina.

When I first realized that mountains as high as the Himalayas resulted from the crash, I thought about standing on the Highland Rim, looking east and seeing the mountains, the way travelers driving north can see the Grand Tetons in Wyoming many miles before reaching them. But, said Dr. Harrison, that's unlikely, even on a clear day, since the peaks were in central and eastern North Carolina.

In the same way that the first and second mountains resulting from the crash eroded away, the *Encyclopedia Britannica* describes the Appalachians we see now as "mere nubbins of what they once were." They could have been lost altogether, but when the supercontinent formed by the collision (called Pangea) split apart and the ocean we call the Atlantic opened, the Appalachians remained part of North America.

17

During all this upheaval, living things kept developing: flora and fauna, fishes, reptiles, birds and mammals. Living things kept on developing even though geologists see evidence that there have been five mass extinctions over some 400 million years, periods when much of what was alive perished as the result of some catastrophic event. (Some scientists think we are now in the sixth period of mass extinctions.) All the while, seas came and went for a long time over parts of Tennessee. Robert Miller writes in his *Geologic History of Tennessee* that some forty million years ago you could have watched whales spout in the seas of west Tennessee "for their bones have been found . . . at Fort Pillow near the mouth of the Hatchie River north of Memphis."

Just over three hundred years ago the English poet Andrew Marvell wrote a poem that begins, "If there were world enough and time. . ." I think there is world enough. It's time that's in short supply for poets and the rest of us. If you pull off the highway just outside of Gainesboro where Roaring River meets the Cumberland, the high limestone cliffs run along the highway. If you pick up a sliver of limestone that erosion has peeled from the cliff—a piece laid down in a shallow sea untold millions of years ago—it's a reminder that a human life is to earth time what the sliver of limestone is to the cliff.

How can one human life have any value in terms of all the billions of human lives, past, present, and still to come? Perhaps it's the brevity of one life that allows us to address how little time we have to value every life, and how little time we have to turn our astonished gaze upon the body of the world.

Sweet Williams &
Stinking Willies

In American history and geography Cumberland is a familiar name.

Just north of Gainesboro the 687-mile Cumberland River, its headwaters in Harlan County, Kentucky, makes a bend to the southwest before looping its way down to Nashville. The Cumberland Plateau includes parts of five states, including Kentucky and Tennessee. The Cumberland Mountains form the southeastern section of the Appalachian range. The Cumberland Gap, a mountain pass used originally by native tribes, became known to Europeans when Dr. Thomas Walker discovered it in 1750 and named it. Located at the juncture of what is now Tennessee, Kentucky and Virginia, it was widened by Daniel Boone and a team of loggers, and by 1796 westward bound settlers drove their wagons through the Gap on an all-weather road.

The Cumberland Narrows is a gorge in northwestern Maryland discovered in 1754. Later, after the Congress authorized funds in 1806 for the first federal highway, it became a part of the National Road, sometimes known as the Cumberland Road and sometimes as the National Pike, which originally linked Cumberland, Maryland, and Wheeling, West Virginia, and is now part of U.S. Interstate 40.

A block of counties in the northeastern area of middle Tennessee is known as the Upper Cumberland. Jackson County, with Gainesboro as the county seat, is of one them. Most Americans know why a county would be named after Andrew Jackson, but not many know the name William Augustus, Duke of Cumberland, son of England's King George II. However, the name provides some reasons for the migration of Scots to the new world in the 18th century. Some of them making the dangerous journey west through the Cumberland Gap must have contemplated the grim irony of it all.

Scotland and Ireland's resentment of English domination meant low level, long-term resistance marked at times by outright war. Sometimes war was meant to settle which group within the English realm would wield power, the kind of disagreement that produces rebellion. One of these conflicts, which off and on lasted from 1689 to 1746, pitted Protestant supporters of England's 1688 Glorious Revolution against supporters of the Stuart king, James II, a Roman Catholic convert. The Glorious Revolution allowed the English Parliament for the first time to depose a king. It replaced James II with the Dutch Protestant William of Orange, who became King William III. Those who remained loyal to James II came to be called Jacobites, Jacobus being Latin for James. As Scotland was home territory for the Stuart dynasty, the Jacobites were strong in Scotland and Wales. In Ireland they found support among Roman Catholics.

Intrigue and war were common. Between 1689 and 1745, the Jacobites and their allies in France, where James II was in exile, and their allies among English Tories made five attempts to restore the Stuart kings to the throne. In 1745, the young Stuart prince, Charles Edward, known as Bonnie Prince Charlie, grandson of James II, landed in Scotland, successfully took the country and even drove into Britain. He retreated to the Scottish Highlands to spend the winter of 1746.

In April the English king, George II, sent his son, William Augustus, Duke of Cumberland, to put down the uprising. This he did, at the Battle of Culloden near Inverness. Some thousand Scots were killed, and some in the Duke's army finished off injured Scots still on the battlefield. The Duke had 120 executed and thousands more hunted down and "wantonly" (says the *Encyclopedia Britannica*) killed or sent into exile. For all this, he was given the nickname "Butcher" Cumberland.

In England, a flower called the "sweet william" is named after him, but some say in Scotland it's called the "stinking willie."

The Battle of Culloden was one of the his few military successes, but it was the battle that finally defeated the Jacobites and made the Duke in Protestant English eyes a man worthy of high honors. So it was that the name of Cumberland, associated so strongly with old European quarrels, is bestowed upon towns, rivers, plateaus, roads, mountains, and mountain passes in the new world.

Their Guns & Their Bibles

Responding to the U.S. Census, most Jackson County residents describe themselves as English, Scots, Irish, or Scots-Irish. It's likely that many of these residents have in their veins some, maybe mostly, Scots-Irish blood. This is true for all the Upper Cumberland counties, as well as East and Middle Tennessee and much of the south.

The migration of what came to be called the Scots-Irish out of Scotland and Ireland—mostly out of Ulster in Northern Ireland in the sixty or so years before the American Revolution—is one of the great journeys out of Europe to the New World. It was a change precipitated by economic hardship and religious dissent, made by a people familiar with hardship and religious persecution.

Centuries before this migration, people called the lowland Scots lived on the northern side of the border established by the wall that the Emperor Hadrian began in 122 AD. The Romans withdrew from Britain as their empire collapsed, but through the centuries this border land remained a disputed territory. In the years after the Normans conquered England—that famous date, 1066—the Norman kings sought to extend

23

their domain. In the latter part of the 13th century, the Norman king Edward I set out to subdue the lowland Scots. His campaigns against them were markedly brutal: for example, on March 30, 1296, he laid waste to the thriving seaport town of Berwick, reportedly killing some 17,000 men, women, and children in a single day.

This display of state terrorism did not subdue the Scots; instead it brought them the next year to open rebellion, led by their most famous hero of this period, William Wallace. A commoner, he was made famous in our time by Mel Gibson's film "Braveheart." Wallace and his band of guerilla fighters had some success against Edward, but in 1305 he was betrayed by Scottish lords supposedly fighting with him against the English, and he was convicted of treason, hanged, disemboweled, his body pulled apart by horses, and his severed head placed on a pike.

Almost ten years later the Scots led by the hero Robert the Bruce did defeat Edward and establish Scotland's right to exist, but political stability eluded the new country, and generations of lowland Scots remained in poverty.

In Ireland, the Catholic Church led by the Jesuit order established a church that earned the allegiance of its adherents. In Scotland, the Church was notoriously corrupt, and there the Protestant Reformation found fertile ground, especially in the lowlands. As the Reformation gathered momentum, religious belief became increasingly politicized and again and again religious disagreement, combined with a nation's territorial, dynastic, or what we today would call "security" needs, led to war. At the beginning of the 17th century, an Irish rebellion centered in the northern area of Ireland called Ulster began. The Irish allied themselves with Catholic Spain, Protestant England's old enemy. The rebellion failed, and the English instituted a scorched earth policy in Ulster and allowed famine to depopulate the area.

Thus the genesis of Ulster Plantation, begun by the English in 1603 to "plant" Protestants in Ulster to counter the Irish Catholics to the south. Most of the migrants hadn't far to go, moving from the Scottish lowlands across the narrow channel of the Irish Sea that separates Scotland from Ireland. In his book *Born Fighting: How the Scots-Irish Shaped America*, James Webb describes these desperately poor migrants as "hard-bitten, unbending, tightly knit lowland Scots." After centuries of border conflict with the British, they were accustomed to warfare and its perils, including having to quickly leave minimal lodgings they called "cabbins" and relocate. Because their experience with those in powerful positions in England and Scotland left them mistrustful of central authority, they gave their allegiance to strong local leaders who proved their worthiness not in commerce or finance, but on the battlefield.

The Protestant belief that the core religious bond is between the individual and God struck a responsive cord in the lowland Scots, for this bond gives individuals not only a moral right but a duty to listen to their conscience and to act without waiting for guidance from a priest, pope, or king. In the stern, unyielding, fundamentalist views of John Calvin and John Knox that centered power in local congregations, they found a religion consistent with what Webb calls their "bottom up" as opposed to "top down" way of being in the world.

Poor but independent, individualistic, stubborn, un-yielding, argumentative, literally and figuratively ready for battle, fundamentalist and congregation-centered in religion, without commitment to any national government—these were the people who migrated to Ulster Plantation. It's not surprising that they clashed with Catholic Ireland or that the conflict inherent in the idea of establishing Ulster Plantation resulted in a brutal struggle that lasted until the end of the 20th century. Also not surprising was that just as they clashed with the Catholics, they also clashed with English and Irish Anglicans, who called themselves "conformist" Protestants. The Anglicans, with their hierarchal church structure, royalist sympathies, and secure social and economic position, had no time for the "nonconformist" Scots.

The mix in Ulster of Scots and English, with the Catholics next door, produced endless discontent. The English civil war that spanned most of the 17th century only added to the misery.* The century saw Charles I beheaded by Oliver

---

*It's hard to under estimate the resentments stirred by religious and civil war. Oliver Cromwell died in 1659 and was buried with great honors in Westminster Abby. In 1661, Royalist supporters exhumed his body and executed it posthumously. They hanged his exhumed body in chains, then threw it into a pit after cutting off the head, which was displayed on a pole in London until 1685. Apparently his head survived after a fashion, and it is reported that eventually one Josiah H.Wilkerson bought it in 1814.

Cromwell and his Roundheads in 1649. Eleven years later in 1660 English citizens saw the Roundheads rejected and Charles II called to the throne. The Catholic James II, crowned in 1685, was ejected by the Parliament in 1688. In an attempt to regain the throne James II led an Irish rebellion known for the months-long siege of Londonderry, a Protestant city in Ulster. The siege was broken after English forces arrived, but far too late to save thousands of lives, some lost by military action, many by disease and starvation.

At the beginning of the 18th century, one hundred years after the establishment of Ulster Plantation, the Protestant English government enforced laws designed to ensure the primacy of the Anglican church. Webb writes, "The 1703 Test Act was specifically aimed at subduing the dominant Presbyterian culture in Ulster, requiring that all office holders in Ireland take the sacrament of the Anglican Church. It also eliminated the legitimacy of Presbyterian ministers, thereby removing the legality of marriage ceremonies, baptisms, and even burial rites."

Thus did couples married by Presbyterian ministers in the eyes of the law "instantly become fornicators . . . and their children were now regarded as bastards. In many parts of Ulster the Presbyterians could not even conduct a burial ceremony unless an Episcopalian minister performed the service." Presbyterians could not teach school, hold government positions, or become officers in the militia. The Scots-Irish were unmoved. If in 1603 they were already known for their "nonconformist" traits, by 1703 they were even more convinced of the correctness of their fundamentalist beliefs.

The lack of religious toleration no doubt fueled Scots-Irish anger and discontent, but it was the general wretchedness of poverty that impacted their daily lives. The poor had no money and no way of getting any. Most hated was "rack renting." Renters worked their fields until their rental period expired, then owners raised rents and rented the land to the highest bidder.

The Test Act and general economic despair set the stage for the Scots-Irish migration out of Ulster. Usually in groups of several hundred, they set sail for the new world across the deepest of oceans. Among their meager belongings they included their guns and their Bibles. From about 1720 to 1775, some half a million left Ulster, nearly all non-conformist Protestants.

Initially, they sought out the Puritans in New England, thinking that their Calvinism would be welcomed there, but the Puritans insisted they become Congregationalists, and besides, they found the newcomers, well, at best, difficult. Webb describes them as "A quick-tempered but sensual and playful people, [who] often dressed provocatively, acted with a volatile belligerence, drank to excess, engaged in constant and open competition in every form, and adamantly defied the attempts of outsiders to control them."

They were not needed in Tidewater Virginia—there slaves labored. Eventually many landed in Pennsylvania, a center of religious tolerance in the colonies. The Quakers there were loath to raise a militia even though they were in danger of Indian attacks. The Scots-Irish, known for their defense of Londonderry and their war experience, were given land west of Philadelphia so that their settlements would act as a buffer against Indian attacks. They provided that protection, but they also began to spread out onto lands not allocated for them. In sum, in this and other ways, the Quakers, like the Congregationalists, came to consider them more troublesome than useful.

In time the emigrants moved west into Kentucky and Tennessee and south into the Carolinas, then into the deep south. They knew how to build a homestead and enlist the family in its defense. The skills they brought from Ulster served them well in the wilderness.

They also brought with them a hatred of the English. It is estimated that they provided the American Revolutionary War with between a third and a half of the rebel forces. Soldiers from "over the mountain" in southwest Virginia, the Carolinas, and east Tennessee destroyed a British army in 1780 at King's Mountain in North Carolina, one of the turning points of the war.

After the war, some stayed in Appalachia, a part of America that has become both a region and a culture and of which the Upper Cumberland is on the far western edge. They retain the characteristics common to their forebears: clannish, intensely competitive in some things but not focused on accumulating wealth, admiring of military service, suspicious of any government not led by locals, fierce in their resentments and in maintaining their prerogatives, contemptuous of those with whom they disagree. In their politics they tend to be populist and sometimes radical, suspicious of "the elites" in government, education, or commerce. They sometimes condone hard-nosed business practice or ignore local corruption, especially if it's a "good ole boy." They remain fundamentalist in their religion.

Not long after the Ulster Scots began their migration, the Enlightenment arrived in Scotland, bringing with it near the end of the century economic and educational change that helped Scotland move into the modern world. Webb writes that "by the 1780's the country would be in an intellectual and commercial 'takeoff,' still rural but having passed a turning point fed by the Industrial Revolution and the advent of the cotton textile industry." The Scots-Irish of Ulster, who out of economic and religious necessity had emigrated, missed "the new schools, new ideas, new possibilities, new hope." They crossed the sea and spearheaded the clearing of a vast wilderness. Textbooks and philosophers were not the survival tools they required.

They had their guns and their Bibles, and these they deemed sufficient.

Steamboat Prosperity
& Civil War Misery

Although Gainesboro has never been a big town, it has seen some good times since it became the county seat of Jackson County just a few years after Andrew Jackson became the nation's hero at the Battle of New Orleans in 1815.

The first good times for Gainesboro began in the early 1830s when steamboats began making their way up the Cumberland River from Nashville. In a remote area of few roads and no railroads, using the river to ship produce and merchandise up stream and down opened profitable markets. Landings were set up at Gainesboro and Celina (twenty miles farther north), and between the two towns, at Butler's Landing, where legend has it Daniel Boone camped in the 1780s.

Through the 1830s, '40s and '50s steamboats plied the upper river, carrying increasing amounts of freight. In his book *Steamboatin' on the Cumberland,* Byrd Douglas writes that the steamboat breakthrough turned the Upper Cumberland into "a veritable steamboat paradise, at times originating more freight than the packets could handle."[1] Byrd describes Gainesboro as a small town with a large steamboat business serving an extensive trade area. Farmers shipped down river a range of products, including tobacco, corn, hogs, furs, hides, poultry, eggs, and timber. Steamboat passengers could take a leisurely three-day trip down to Nashville, then make their way to the Mississippi and take a steamboat to cities like St. Louis or New Orleans.

The War Between the States put an end to that first steamboat prosperity. By the early summer of 1861 the steamboat business on the Cumberland and the other western rivers "was a thing of the past,"[3] according to Byrd. In the struggle over control of the Cumberland River the Union gained the advantage and used the river to ship supplies to its army. Union gunboats dominated the countryside.

In 1860 the population of Jackson County (which at that time included Clay and Putnam counties) totaled 11,725. Just over 10,000 were white, 46 were free blacks, and 1,212 were slaves. In the June, 1861 secession vote 1,483 of Jackson County's eligible males voted to secede, and just over 700 voted against. Thus in Jackson County, as in other Upper Cumberland counties, the war split communities and families, "county by county, farm by farm. The normal forms of governance disintegrated."[4] As a result, although the Union had the river advantage, on land there was no peace. While no armies met on a battlefield, the forested hill and hollow terrain invited guerilla warfare, and quick, deadly ambushes served both sides well.[5] Moreover, says Moldon J. Tayse in her history of Jackson County, some "seized the opportunity the war provided to rob and destroy, settle previous grievances, and murder."[6] Those who chose no side found themselves suspected by each side's partisans.

In April of 1863, Union troops landed in Celina, (which, like Gainesboro, was a center of Rebel support), shelled and burned the town and killed some ninety Confederates. "The entire town, save only four houses, was demolished."[7] In 1864 Union gunboats landed 1,000 troops in Jackson County. In the same year, Old Columbus, a town a mile just north of Gainesboro at the confluence of the Cumberland and Roaring rivers, was burned.

In his essay, "Fevers Ran High," included in *Rural Life and Culture in the Upper Cumberland,* James B. Jones, Jr., recounts the misery the war inflicted upon the area. Lawlessness and anarchy prevailed. Both sides confiscated supplies—grain, livestock, food, whatever was wanted or needed—from their enemies' supporters, who tended to be Union if they were small farmers, Rebel if they were larger landowners and elected officials. Either way, the plundering of the Upper Cumberland was ruthlessly extensive. Jones writes that "the combined efforts of Yankees and Rebels heaped... suffering on the Upper Cumberland's citizenry."[8] By 1864, some areas were nearing famine, with those formerly wealthy wiped out and the poor starving.

The moment to moment intensity of war—times when life, death, and the future hang in the balance—command the interest of novelists, biographers, historians, and readers. How regions, communities, and individuals rebuild themselves after the war—often that's just seen as a long, slow business that gets done somehow, some way. The Upper Cumberland's divisions and hardships would delay its adjustment to the peace that came in the spring of 1865. According to Jones, "many a memory sustained the devastation, causing hatred to burst forth sporadically, manifesting itself in a variety of killings into the next century."[8] Moldon describes the postwar time in Jackson County as "years of strife and gloom."[9]

Conflict between whites, black freemen, and former slaves added to the postwar tension. With emancipation former slaves became free citizens, and in the years following the war, a small African American community established itself in Gainesboro. Nowhere, however did the freedom of the former slaves translate into social and political equality. Decade by decade the scourge of official racism grew, culminating in the South in the adoption of Jim Crow laws and across the nation in a general acceptance of racist views.

Enforcing inequality with violence was common. In "Slavery, Freedom, and Citizenship," an essay in *Rural Life and Culture in the Upper Cumberland*, Wali R. Kharif reviews a survey by the NAACP documenting lynchings between 1889 and 1918. In Tennessee, of 190 deaths 155 were freedmen ("...some were hanged, others shot, dragged to death or burned at the stake"[10]). Four occurred in the Upper Cumberland, none recorded in Jackson or Clay counties. One of the lynched was a white man, for rape; one a black woman, Ballie Crutchfield, for theft. [11]

There was, however, in 1894 in Gainesboro, the hanging of Fate Ritchie, a black man accused of the robbery and murder of a white man, Bill Stephens. After his arrest he had to be taken to the jail in Nashville to protect his life. Ritchie claimed innocence up to the moment of his death, and it was reported that even Stephens' wife believed him falsely charged. His hanging drew thousands of onlookers to the town, although the scaffold and hanging, which was botched, were fenced off from the view of the crowd.[12]

Such events and their aftermath partly (or perhaps mostly) explain why the Upper Cumberland, including Gainesboro and Jackson County, is now largely an all-white region. In addition, historians today document turn-of-the-century racial evictions by white southern communities. One occurred around 1910 at Lafayette in Macon County, just north of Gainesboro. Tension was such that black residents, then thirteen percent of the population, were given an ultimatum to leave town, and Kharif writes that whites "detonated half a stick of dynamite in the yard of each black resident. . . .An exodus followed, with blacks leaving their property behind."[13]

Some went to Gravel Hill in Macon County, one of three all-black settlements in the area; the other two were Tate Town in Cumberland County, and Free Hill, just northeast of Celina in Clay County. The settlements (which had been established before the Civil War) provided some solace and peace, along with schools, businesses, churches, and community entertainment.

Fortunately, resentments, economic hardship, and racial tension were not the whole postwar story. By 1870, river traffic "had developed the Upper Cumberland territory into one of the richest and most lucrative trade areas on the Western Rivers,"[14] according to Douglas in *Steamboatin' on the*

Cumberland. From Nashville up to Burnside, Kentucky, river trade totaled millions. William Lynwood Montell in his book *Don't Go Up Kettle Creek* says shipping material via the river proved more convenient than hauling it to and from a railroad station—by the late 1880s only Cookeville in the Upper Cumberland could be considered a real railroad town. Included in hundreds of thousands of pounds of raw materials shipped by boat to Nashville were tobacco, grains, lumber, whiskey, animals, hardware, meats, furs, and flour. Upstream goods included drugs, clothing, furniture, hardware, wagons, saddles, snuff, coffee, and items ordered from Sears, Roebuck and Company, including a prefabricated house shipped piece by piece.[15]

But the big new thing was timber. The national building boom that began after the Civil War made timber a product in high demand, and counties like Jackson, Clay, and Overton had millions of acres of cedar, oak, ash, poplar, beech, walnut, and hickory trees. The cutting of Upper Cumberland timber began around 1870, with its heyday between 1890 and 1912. Initially, the timber was sent downstream by steamboat, but over time loggers found it more efficient to tie logs together, creating huge rafts that were floated down to Nashville, which became one of the largest lumber centers in the country. As a regional center, Gainesboro was part of a chain.

Rafting logs down river was a dangerous business, but like so much of river life, also exhilarating, and Upper Cumberland men like Cordell Hull, who became a famous Secretary of State in President Franklin Roosevelt's administration, and John Gore, who became a U. S. District Judge, gained legendary status as raftsmen.

However, trees don't grow on trees, to coin a phrase, and by 1915, "The giant trees within reasonable distance of the rivers were gone and the boom days were over,"[16] says Montell in *Don't Go Up Kettle Creek*. The Great Depression ruined the Nashville timber market, and over time, log rafting on the Cumberland became the stuff of memory and fable.

The last steamboat to ply the Upper Cumberland left the river in 1928.

Sources

Birdwell, Michael E, and W. Calvin Dickinson, eds. *Rural Life and Culture in the Upper Cumberland*. Lexington: University Press of Kentucky, 2004.

Douglas, Byrd, *Steamboatin' on the Cumberland*. Nashville: Tennessee Book Company, 1961.

Dudley, Bob, *Those Were the Days,* available in the Tennessee Archives in Nashville in the Jackson County section.

Keith, Jeanette, *County People in the New South: Tennessee's Upper Cumberland*. Chapel Hill: University of North Carolina Press, 1995.

Montell, William Lynwood, *Don't Go Up Kettle Creek: Verbal Legacy of the Upper Cumberland*. Knoxville: University of Tennessee Press, 1983.

Tayse, Moldon, *Jackson County Tennessee*. Tennessee State Library and Archives: Nashville, 1989.

Notes

1. Byrd Douglas, *Steamboatin' on the Cumberland,* (Tennessee Book Company, 1961), p.59.

2. Ibid., p.102

3. Slavery was not widespread in the Upper Cumberland, as the region's hill and valley terrain does not lend itself to plantation farming. In conversation with Therold Richardson (see "Therold Richardson's Journey") he related that his great-grandfather owned slaves, and during the Civil War hid them from Union troops who would, Richardson said he was told, have killed them. I wondered about this fear of Union soldiers and asked Robert Hunt, history professor at MTSU, if there was historical evidence for this.

In an email, he replied, "Not that I'm aware of. I think what you DO run into is that the soldiers in the Union army came from all different kinds of backgrounds. There was not united North that fought a united South. Rather, the Union fought the Confederacy, and this Union was composed of many different groups. In the Army of the Cumberland, which is what I study, you had 14 regiments from Kentucky (at least with that state label), several regiments of Midwesterners the members of which were Democrats, and some attached troops from East Tennessee. Then add your Lincoln Republicans. Every 'racial' opinion you could want (or not want) was represented in the Union army. There were plenty of Union soldiers who had, as they put it, "no love for the Negro," but you also had intense abolitionists in the arny as well.

Within this tremendous variation of attitudes, the soldiery shifted their view of blacks during the war. At first (1861) most of the men would say that they had signed up to fight the secessionists not liberate the slaves. However, as time went on they noticed that: (a) the slaves who tried to escape to their lines brought not only their labor but useful information; (b) slaves represented a huge labor supply that could be shifted from working for the Confederacy to working for the Union. It was also the case that slaves often greeted Union soldiers as liberators. I've never known any group of American soldiers who didn't soak up being greeted as angels of mercy. In short, Union soldiers came to have every reason to see blacks as tacit 'allies,' and many, even most did so.

From this point, however, the usual realities of war intruded. Slaves seeking liberation were incorporated into the army as a work force (contraband), and in these situations they were often either mistreated or plainly neglected.

Long story short, there are some truly ugly stories that come out of the Union soldiery's encounters with slaves and aspiring freed people. However, I'm not aware of anything unique in this regard compared to any of America's other wars. In any situation like this there are opportunities for neglect and abuse, and these things occurred. This understood, Union troops for the most part were smart enough to figure out who their friends were in this big fight. Many also came to have real, genuine sympathy for this group of people whom they regarded as being caught in the middle of a nasty war. At the same time, you also had individual Union soldiers who were abusive because they were abusive to anybody. Thus, Southern families who "hid" their slaves—or said they were—weren't hiding them to protect them, they were trying to prevent their property from running away. As well, Union soldiers—most of them—were bright enough to figure out that slaves were a useful resource in a mean, long, bloody war."

In a subsequent email, he wrote, "I should add that one of the E Tennessee mounted regiments raised under governor Andrew Johnson's authority (I believe) did go to Gallatin Tn and threaten to murder all the black refugees staying there. In particular they were incensed by the idea that the refugees (some of them) were receiving literacy instruction."

4. Jeanette Keith, *County People of the New South: Tennessee's Upper Cumberland* (University of North Carolina Press, 1995), p. 8.

5. Moldon J. Tayse, *Jackson County Tennessee,* 1989, p. 60.

6. James B. Jones, Jr., "Fevers Ran High," in *Rural Life and Culture in the Upper Cumberland,* eds. Michael E Birdwell and W. Calvin Dickinson, (University Press of Kentucky, 2004), p. 86.

7. Ibid.

8. Ibid., p. 101.

9. Tayse, *Jackson County Tennessee,* p. 67.

10. Wali R. Kharif, "Slavery, Freedom, and Citizenship," in *Rural Life and Culture in the Upper Cumberland,* eds. Michael E Birdwell and W. Calvin Dickinson, (University Press of Kentucky, 2004), p. 109.

11. Ibid.

12. Ibid.

13. Kharif, "Slavery, Freedom and Citizenship," p. 111.

14. Douglas, *Steamboatin' on the Cumberland,* p. 176.

15. William Lynwood Montell, *Don't Go Up Kettle Creek: Verbal Legacy of the Upper Cumberland (* University of Tennessee Press, 1983), p.134.

16. Ibid. p.118.

Therold Richardson's Journey

Therold Richardson's insurance and real estate office occupied a center spot on Gore Street directly across from the south door of the Jackson County Courthouse. A steep roof adorned with a decorative white shingled triangle, a window with white shutters, and white columns in front of the door gave the entry a cottage look. Inside, the office turned out to be larger than it appeared from the street. In the first of the dark-paneled rooms the secretary and receptionist, Mrs. Jones, held sway; behind her area was Richardson's office. There, on a table beside a chair for guests he'd placed a copy of *Blue Grass Music in the Upper Cumberland,* a book that includes a chapter called "The Singing Mayor: The Musical Career of Therold Richardson."

In the hallway a large bulletin board held photographs, thank you notes, and mementos, including a pamphlet featuring a black and white close-up of Lyndon Johnson handed out at a fund raiser when Johnson was a candidate for president and Richardson was Gainesboro's mayor. The hall led to a large back room lined with shelves holding more books, souvenirs, and photos. A photograph of him when he was probably in his mid-forties showed him with his guitar, wearing a suit and not smiling and heftier then. In his mid-eighties he was a slender, upright man, with white hair, blue eyes, and a humor marked by the gentle irony of one who had lived and worked among people he had always known and mostly appreciated. He was still singing, and each Tuesday night invited musicians to join him in the back room for several hours of picking and singing. Some were Richardson's age, a few were high school students, most somewhere in between.

Centuries ago the Persian poet Rumi wrote, "Notice how everyone has just arrived here from a journey." When Richardson and I sat down at his tan utilitarian office desk in the back room, I asked him about his journey and about Gainesboro's. When he was a child and even into mid-life, Gainesboro was the center of a busy rural community. Through the 1940s and the next few decades, Saturdays brought shoppers from outlying areas to the square. They came to buy groceries and clothes, have lunch at one of the cafes, stop for a fountain drink at one of two drug stores, check out the new models at local car dealerships, and, of course, visit and watch, as my father used to say, all the funny people.

That was then. Around two o'clock on a summer Saturday afternoon in the middle of the first decade of the 21st century, Richardson told me, "There wasn't a single soul on these streets."

WHEN THEROLD RICHARDSON was born in 1924, neither steamboats nor rafting nor rail had a future in the Upper

Cumberland. Richardson's beginning coincided with another era, that time when the car and the highway had begun to capture America's energy and imagination. By 1930 Tennessee was completing a network of main highways, and the bridge built across the Cumberland just north of town was one of many.

Although Richardson was a child of the Upper Cumberland, his life was changed by events far from home. His father, James Monroe Richardson, was injured in France in World War I when a shell blew up in his camp. He came home in 1919, but his injury, said his son, "affected him in many ways."

On his return from France, James married Lora Carver, and the couple settled at Sugar Creek, six miles north of Gainesboro. There Therold Richardson grew up and, along with some sixty other children, attended the two-room grade school in session from July to March. The community believed it had good teachers, but, as is often the case, how much or how little a student learned tended to be an individual matter.

"I took the eighth grade twice," recalled Richardson. "The first year my teacher was a Mr. Dudney. The first day of school he said, 'I'm here to teach you if you want to learn, but if you don't, that's up to you.'" Richardson laughed and said, "That's all I wanted to hear him say. My books never came out of the book satchel." This Huckleberry Finn interlude ceased when Richardson took the annual achievement test in Gainesboro. "I flunked it."

The next year he walked the two miles back and forth

to school every school day. He kept the certificate awarded him for perfect attendance and said with remembered pleasure, "That year I made the highest grades in the county in the eighth grade." All of this he attributed to his teacher, Miss Vanhooser, who set up a system that awarded students merits for the quality of their work and allowed them to redeem the merits at a little store she kept. "That had an amazing effect on all of us," he said.

By 1930, the Great Depression, plague like, had settled over the country. Richardson's family was especially hard hit when in 1935 the wounds his father James suffered in WWI finally left him unable to continue his life at home. He entered the Veteran's Hospital in Murfreesboro; he never left it and died there in 1962. Richardson, two older brothers, a sister, and his mother lived with her father on his Sugar Creek farm. The brothers helped with the farming and hired out as farm hands. His mother received no state or federal help until 1940, and in the years between 1935 and 1940, Richardson recalled, "We lived one day at a time."

When he was fourteen, Richardson began working for Elmer Swan, owner of a Ford Model T truck distinguished by chicken coops attached to its roof. Swan's "peddlin' truck" took him and the fourteen-year old boy—chickens squawking in their coops—on gravel roads through Jackson County's hills and hollows. In summer, said Richardson, the truck raised such clouds of dust "you couldn't see for about ten minutes after it passed." The day always began at Sugar Creek, but each route was different. It was sun up to sun down work, for which the boy earned 25 to 50 cents a day.

"It was an amazing business. People would wait for that peddlin' truck," said Richardson. "That's the only way the majority of people had of even getting sugar, flour, things of that sort." Swan sold household goods and staples and bought farm produce—eggs, chickens, hams, small animal furs. "If he bought chickens, I had to put the chickens in the coops; if he bought eggs, I had to count 'em." Sometimes there was money exchanged, sometimes there was an even trade—the farmers and their wives "had it figured pretty close." In Richardson's memory Swan's biggest customers were the Mabrys, a family living up Roaring River, who were sometimes the last stop after a long day on the road.

Like World War II veterans, fewer and fewer of those who endured the Great Depression remain to tell their stories, but listeners hearing their accounts find that shared experiences helped dull the impact of hard times. In the Upper Cumberland, like most of Appalachia, blue grass and gospel music were then and are now central to expressing the joy of living and the pain of loss and change.

At the same time Richardson faced the loss of his father and the need to help support his family, he was learning to play the guitar. Just about the time he got his certificate for perfect school attendance, he sold enough mail-order garden seeds to win a guitar. He learned the basics from his brothers and was good enough to attract the attention of older musicians like local favorite Otha Spivey. Spivey lived on the other side of the Cumberland from the Richardsons. To get there for an evening of music, Richardson took himself and his guitar down the river in a canoe, walked a mile up river to Spiveys, played till bedtime, walked back to the canoe, paddled across the river, and walked home.

By the late 1930s Richardson had moved up from walking to peddling a bicycle. Eventually, he swapped it and $10 for a Model T Ford convertible. Gas was eleven cents a gallon. In 1939, he was playing guitar in a band led by Frazier Moss, also from Sugar Creek, who many years later became a national fiddling champion. The band had a four-year stand Saturday mornings on Cookeville's WHUB radio station. No pay, and each had to buy his fifty-cent bus fare to Cookeville. But no matter; the thrill was playing music for thirty minutes on the air every Saturday morning. Who could ask for more?

The two continued playing together until Moss died in 1998. Richardson said that as they grew older, he and Moss would sometimes go out to Sugar Creek, mostly deserted, find a shady spot and play for an hour or so. No audience; just the pleasure of playing.

A high school football knee injury kept him out of the armed services upon graduation in 1943, so he headed north, first to Akron, Ohio, to a job in a rubber plant and then on to a factory job in Detroit, job heaven for Tennesseans. In the spring of 1946, Richardson returned to Gainesboro for what he thought would be a quick four-day trip. The four days included a Sunday in May. Tennessee in May can be a pretty enticing place. In addition, some friends had gathered a softball team together. Richardson played with the team that Sunday. "They started beggin' me to stay," he said, then added, "I probably didn't need a whole lot of persuading." He sent to Detroit for his few belongings.

After living through over a decade of economic depression followed by wartime rationing and scarcity, Americans must have felt in the years following WWII as if a door long closed had swung open at last, allowing them to walk into the Land of Plenty. Tens of thousands sent abroad to fight the war were lost forever, but America's cities, her businesses, factories, farms and towns, unlike many of those in Europe and the Far East, remained intact. Richardson remembers a 1940s Gainesboro with four auto dealerships, five dry goods stores, five doctors, two drugstores and five grocery stores, all on or near the square. It was "almost one hundred percent a farming community," he said, and on the Saturdays that businesses sponsored drawings and give-a-ways as many as 1,500 people from the surrounding community came into town in their cars. Farmers no longer had to wait for Elmer Swan's peddlin' truck.

Initially, Richardson opened a recreation hall and billiard parlor—at the time a preferred enterprise for many a young man. However, in 1949 he married Jean Watson, a Jackson County girl he'd met in the mid-1940s,* and by 1950 he had moved into insurance and real estate. Almost 60 years later, he commented, "I'm still trying to plug at it."

---

*They have one son, Lee, a lawyer, who serves as a city judge in Gainesboro.

His stint as The Singing Mayor began in the spring of 1964; he framed the first check for $25 the town paid him for his time. His tenure coincided with Lyndon's Johnson's Great Society, whose programs provided grants for local improvements, some for one hundred percent of costs, some for fifty percent. Gainesboro got new sewer, gas and water lines. An airport and a golf course (which, Richardson noted slyly, was funded at one hundred percent) were built on land near the Cumberland River and leased for ninety-nine years from the Corps of Engineers. Another project he helped start, the Poke Sallet Festival, made its first appearance on the square in 1977 and remains Gainesboro's main spring event.

The town retained its central place in Jackson County through the 1960s and part of the 1970s, although businesses like the auto dealerships and grocery stores began to fade. The 1980s accelerated the downward trend that has afflicted not just Gainesboro but so much of rural America over the last thirty years. Small farmers that had been the foundation of rural communities like Gainesboro's found themselves less and less able to make a living farming. Some lost their land, some sold out, some sought a better life in cities or suburbs. Some were able to consolidate holdings, but the result of all the change was reduced populations in rural areas. Jackson County's population in 1940 was just over 15,000; by 1950, just over 12,000. The 2010 census shows a population increase between 2000 and 2010 of over six percent, to 11,683. However, in the same decade, private non-farm employment dropped by 26.5 percent.

On my first visit to the Jackson County courthouse, I talked with some officials and employees. I mentioned that on my travels I had seen many small towns like Gainesboro struggling to survive. When I asked the source of Gainesboro's decline, one woman said, "Walmart," then she amended that to "No, it was before that, it was K-Mart."

The K-Marts and Walmarts thrive in Cookeville, twenty miles to the southeast, but what sparked Cookeville's current growth was a highway. From the National Highway envisioned by the country's eighteenth century founders to Route 66, roads through the wilderness and across the nation's vast plains have changed America, and none more than the interstate highway system. I-40 rolls across the continent from ocean to ocean, each year carrying millions of travelers and eighteen-wheelers loaded with cargo. Located on I-40 midway between Nashville and Knoxville, Cookeville became the town with the big chain stores and restaurants and all the attendant services and employment. It keeps growing; someday, predicted Richardson, "Gainesboro will be a suburb of Cookeville."

Business expansion and consolidation became and remains a dominant trend. Banks offer a ready example. Once locally owned, most banks are now part of regional or national chains. Gainesboro has two regional banks, and in Cookeville, Richardson pointed out, "There's a bank on every corner, " a phenomenon observable in towns on the upswing. Although Gainesboro's banks are no longer locally owned, "They do a good job here," he said.

In the ever accelerating real estate and lending boom

49

of the 2000s, banks loosened their lending policies. "Back in the good old days," said Richardson, "it took three signatures to get a note signed. Now, they don't care if you've got a signature or not. If you've got anything to back it up, they'll lend you any amount of money, especially on farm land." It may have been the real estate man in him who spoke when he said, "Today, they'll loan you one hundred percent on one hundred or ten thousand acres, no collateral needed. That's a big, big help." [*]

In addition to his insurance and real estate business, Richardson established an auction business—he said he'd "sold nearly everything in this county one time or another at auction"—and one of the biggest changes he saw was the huge increase in the value of private and commercial property. He recalled a house and ten acres in Cookeville that before I-40 sold for $8,500. Currently, the same property, the site of a K-mart store that is part of a shopping center near I-40, is worth millions. In the 1950s farm land commonly sold for $25 an acre; now the cheapest farm land is $2,000 to $5,000 an acre. However, buying land at that price and making a living farming it can be an uphill prospect. Having a good-sized cattle herd helps, said Richardson, and, once again, harvesting timber provides income.

In the early years of the new century newcomers from

---

*Richardon made his comments before it became apparent in 2007-08 that "no collateral needed" had turned into a big, big problem.

states like Florida arrived. They found paying $5,000 for an acre of land "a steal," said Richardson, and paying $110,000 for a five-acre lot on a rock bluff overlooking a lake seemed perfectly reasonable. "They buy property sight unseen," marveled Richardson. "They've got so much money they need to do something with it. I don't know if they're dodging taxes or what. It's unreal."*

While some of those new to the area are awash in money, local working people who depended on local manufacturing jobs saw many of those jobs disappear. Decades ago, tax breaks and the prospect of low wages brought manufacturers to the area, but cheaper wages—usually many dollars cheaper—are now found abroad. Two manufacturing firms just outside Gainesboro had shifted or were preparing to shift all or part of their manufacturing business to Mexico or China. Richardson said that he was acquainted with one worker whose company intends to send him to China for training, whereas once the company might have brought Chinese workers to Gainesboro. In another change, construction-related work and the kind of farmhand jobs Richardson and his brothers did to tide the family over in the 1930s are now done mainly by low-paid Mexican and Central American laborers who send their meager wages to families in their own countries.

However, Gainesboro found itself of interest to investors who had millions at their disposal. Richardson recalled

---

*The crash of the housing market in Florida and elsewhere ended the local housing boom.

one visitor to his office who'd sold property in the Florida Keys and "owns about half the town now. He's got hopes. He's doing a lot of improvements and I wish him well, but at the present time I can't see where his business and income are going to come from."

Revitalizing the fading center of towns like Gainesboro has tempted some investors, but the kinds of businesses that used to anchor the town square have moved down to Highway 56. "We call it 'the strip,'" grinned Richardson. That's where shoppers find grocery stores, cafes, filling stations, and the only fast food franchise in town, the Dairy Queen, an enterprise that illustrates the degree of change. Richardson recalled that the man who put it in expected to make at least $650,000 the first year just from the drive through, and, in fact, exceeded his goal.

"Notice how everyone has just arrived here from a journey," wrote the Persian poet Rumi centuries ago. Therold Richardson's journey began as a Sugar Creek farm child in the 1920s with a father ill from the effects of a WW I shell. In the Great Depression he spent long, dusty days riding in Elmer Swan's peddlin' truck and nights playing guitar at Otha Spivey's house. As a young man he sought wartime work up north, then, back in Tennessee, enjoyed a long baseball summer.

In Gainesboro he found family and postwar prosperity and for over fifty years watched the changes that came to the town. His journey took him to Gainesboro's empty square on a Saturday afternoon, not what he would have preferred in the 21st century, but, in his own life, he had seen the range of possibilities time can offer.

The Circle

Therold Richardson was 84 when I first interviewed him in his Gainesboro real estate office. He was so articulate and so interested in the world around him that I forgot something important: When you're eighty-four years old, time offers no guarantees.

In the meantime, however, knowing him allowed me as a listener to enjoy occasionally his Tuesday night music sessions in the back room of his office on Gainesboro's square. Sometimes high school or college students joined in, but mostly it was men (I saw only a few women) and mostly they were grey beards, although Richardson had at least a decade or two on the regulars.

They would arrive, lay their cases in the hall, take out their guitars, or sometimes a mandolin or banjo. It seemed that just the act of retrieving their instruments, sometimes classic and expensive, sometimes just a favorite, was part of the pleasure of the evening. Richardson would have arranged seven or eight chairs in a circle and for a few hours they'd sing and play. He sat in front of his desk, his small tape recorder to his left, and recorded every song. There were sometimes a few listeners, wives or drop-in visitors like me, who sat just outside the circle on a couch Richardson placed against a brown paneled wall.

This scene with players forming a circle is timeless and universal. Richardson and his fellow musicians played many of the same gospel songs each week— "Will the Circle Be Unbroken," "I'll Fly Away," "We Will Gather at the River" —and Richardson often sang in his still strong tenor, "It's Me Again, Lord." Bluegrass favorites were "Blue Moon of Kentucky" and just about any Bill Monroe song. There was usually some Hank Williams, some contemporary country, and some of the patriotic songs made famous by country stars.

Richardson's Tuesday circle was not, however, his only music project. Every second Saturday of the month a local crowd gathered in a big room attached to the now empty Fox School to hear who was playing at the "Little Opry." Performers might be area instrumentalists, bands, family groups, singers, trios, duos—performers Richardson found and thought would please the listeners.

Audience and musicians often knew one another and exchanged friendly banter. There was no charge, but the hat got passed, and sometimes someone used the Little Opry to make a major contribution. Going through the proceeds after the November 2009 gathering, Richardson found a check for $10,000 made out to St. Jude's Children's Hospital, another of his interests.

He wasn't feeling well in November. "I've been doing this for ten years," he said a little wearily. Still, the Little Opry was his baby and his responsibility. Sometimes when he didn't feel like he felt ten years ago, that responsibility felt heavy, but that didn't mean he was ready to give it up. At the December gathering he told the crowd that there would be no Little Opry until April of 2010 due to building repairs. Standing at the microphone, seeming tired and perhaps in pain, his face drawn, Richardson asked for a show of hands as to how many would be back in April, and a hundred or so hands shot up.

Those hands indicated the value the people there put on the Little Opry and help explain why it exists at all. It's not a likely step up the ladder to fame and fortune. It's not held to court someone's favor. Richardson didn't break any molds creating it. It exists because he and they cared about its being, and its creation helps bring together a community of people who love this kind of American music.

I had thought that the Little Opry might cease after Richardson's death on March 17th, 2010, but I noticed in the Jackson County *Sentinel* for February, 2011, that the gathering, now called Therold's Little Opry, still draws a crowd on the second Saturday of the month.

Poke Sallet

I thought my father, born in North Carolina in 1900, spoke of poke "salad" when in New Mexico he lovingly recalled this early spring southern dish. But he may have said poke "sallet," which is an old English term for greens. Back in the day, as people say now, a winter without much in the way of fresh greens must have made poke, a leafy plant that shoots up in early spring, not only a way to clean out a body's winter sludge but a harbinger of the salad season to come.

Jackson County and Gainesboro have been holding their three-day Poke Sallet Festival the second weekend in May since 1971. I went into Gainesboro on a Saturday, figuring that would be the big day. I had thought the crowd at the town's Memorial Day ceremony I'd attended was commendable, but for the Festival every available parking space around the square or anywhere close was filled. I followed Hull Street up the hill, parked across from the Baptist Church, and walked down to the square where shoppers wandered by booths stocked with the usual caps, belt buckles, t-shirts, and trinkets. Kids flocked to carnival rides set up just south of the square.

A puff of smoke on the east side of the square led me to

surmise a meat smoker, and I headed toward the puff. I was seated with other diners at a table under a big umbrella and fully enjoying my pulled pork with barbecue sauce on a bun when Nan, the woman who had served me, took a break from a hot job.

Carrying a plate of poke sallet a neighbor had brought her, she joined the group under the umbrella. "I love it," she said. When I asked about its preparation, she began with, "Well, first, you know, poke is poisonous" (which I didn't know), "so that's why it has to be boiled in water and drained until the water comes clear." She added that it's usually seasoned with bacon drippings and salt, then finished off with an egg scrambled into the cooked greens. The taste, she said, is "a little like spinach but better when it's cooked right." She described the poke sallet the City Cafe up the street was serving as "pretty good," so I decided to give it a try.

On my way to the other side of the square I stopped to talk with a nice looking man probably in his early forties — black hair, blue eyes, a neatly trimmed beard. He'd laid out his collectibles beneath the red and green Coca-Cola advertisement painted on the brick wall of what had been W. T. Reed Groceries at the corner of Main and Hull Street. The corner grocery is long gone, but the city (or somebody) keeps the ad painted. The man included in his items his ex-wife's wedding dress. "That's *ex-wife's*," he stressed. Through the plastic window of a large gold-colored cardboard box I could see a neatly folded white gown, its satin bodice decorated with pearls. "Cost me $350 new," he said, "and worn once." He said they'd divorced in 1988; that meant he'd waited nineteen years to sell the dress she left behind.

I passed the flower shop's display of brightly colored plastic bouquets set out in preparation for Memorial Day. Replaced year after year, the bouquets brighten Tennessee cemeteries. It's a custom strange to me, so different from the spare prairie cemeteries I grew up with in New Mexico.

A full house had set the City Cafe buzzing. I slipped into a just emptied booth nearest the plate glass window facing the street. I hesitated briefly before ordering a dish that at some point had been poisonous, but decided to trust that the cook could see well enough to know when the water ran clear. The small bowl of poke sallet arrived right away and tasted like spinach that needed more seasoning—perhaps bacon drippings, which, let's face it, makes almost anything taste better. Maybe that's what Nan meant when she said it was "pretty good."

Just outside the window was a booth providing information about the Sons of the Confederacy. Most people passed by; one middle-aged couple stopped and talked to the couple in the booth, and the man there apparently wrote up something for them. He wore a T-shirt with the likeness of Nathan Bedford Forrest on it and had grown a long beard like Forrest's, although his was gray. In fact, the image of Forrest was central to the display in the booth. I wasn't sure what to make of that. On leaving the City Cafe, I considered stopping at the Confederate booth to learn its purpose, but wasn't sure how I'd start a conversation, so I passed by.

Still thinking about the man who kept his ex-wife's wedding dress for almost twenty years and about Forrest, remembered in part for being a great Confederate general and in part for being a founder of the KKK (which by some accounts he later rejected), I stopped to sample some muscadine grape cider from the Rock Pile Farm in Grundy County, close to Chattanooga.

There I met Sam, who, although he looked years younger, told me right away that he was eighty-two. "People talk to me about the 'good ole days,' " he said. "I remember when roads around this square weren't paved and there were no electric lights. That didn't happen until 1942. They don't know. Would you like to have to make your own soap?" Glad to find common ground, I said, "Absolutely not." He remembered the time when steamboats plied the Cumberland and spoke disapprovingly of the logging that in the early part of the century brought in cash money but quickly depleted its source.

He continued, " I never saw a colored here when I was growing up." I hadn't anticipated the remark or heard clearly "colored," so I said "What?" Then, in a low voice, he used the N word. "Well," I said, "it's certainly all white here now. I read that African-Americans" — here our eyes met briefly — "were brought in as slaves when the area was settled, but most left after the war."

"The first one I saw," he said, "was one hired as a cook by a man who had a road contracting job around here. When that was over, he was hired on as a cook on one of the steamboats, and I think held that job for as long as he lived."

Sam said his family came to Jackson County from Louisiana. I told him I'd once lived in LaFourche Parish, southwest of New Orleans, in the heart of Cajun country. "Why are they rebuilding that New Orleans area?" he asked. "When those seas rise, it's all going to be all for nothing." I was interested to hear some credence given to global warming in an area where attitudes about it seem to range largely from ridicule to mild resistance.

When a friend came up to greet him, I headed toward the sound of bluegrass. On the sidewalk in front of Therold Richardson's real estate office was a booth filled with guitars, banjos, mandolins, and various paraphernalia musicians need, or maybe just think they need. Behind the booth on the sidewalk were three men seated on folding chairs, one playing a mandolin and two playing guitars, both singers. Behind them two women sang back-up.

I joined a small group listening to some bluegrass, some gospel, and some Hank Williams honky-tonk. They were no doubt pleased to have a few listeners gathered around them, but attracting an audience was not central to their intent, which was to savor being together and making their music. I asked one of the guitar players if they knew any Jimmy Rodgers songs; I thought they'd probably launch right into "T for Texas, T for Tennessee" or "TB Blues," but after some hesitation and tuning up, they rendered a Rodgers love song I'd never heard.

The listeners included Aaron Hammonds, who after we'd talked a while said in a gentle, sympathetic way, "You're not from this part of the country, are you?" I wasn't sure whether it was something acceptable or something just generally un-satisfactory about me that led him to that remark. He did tell me that the guitar player who sang the Jimmy Rodgers song knew "everything thing there was to know about this kind of music," and that little towns in the area would be holding gather-ings like the Poke Sallet Festival throughout the summer. Hammonds also told me that starting at six the band he played with would be performing bluegrass, country, and gospel on the bandstand on the other side of the square. I made plans to go.

At five o'clock the "push an outhouse up a hill" contest was to commence. Jackson County is likely the only place in the world that holds a contest where the winner is the fastest pusher of an outhouse up Hull Street. The flyer for the event said the racing outhouses were made especially for the con-test. I skipped it. I shouldn't have, but I did.

The evening brought relief from the heat. By the time I arrived back at the west end of the square a little after six, the crowd, which filled up the block, had settled into their lawn chairs, fully ready for a spring evening devoted to picking and singing. I found a seat near the lighted bandstand just as Hammonds' group was finishing "Corina, Corina." I think, I may be wrong, but I think I heard the band referred to as the Greasy Creek band.

They were the first of three bands that evening;

Hammonds was a lead singer and played one of two guitars in the band, filled out by a banjo, a bass, and a woman singer. Generally, as in most genres, bluegrass bands are a guy thing; but that night there were two women playing bass fiddle. Another guy thing is bantering with the crowd; Hammonds singled out a man he knew and told a joke about a man and his wife, ending with the line, "You've just got him spoiled, ain't you," and the wife replies, "No, he just smells that way!"

They sang some of the sentimental oldies, like "Wildflowers on Her Grave" and some gospel songs warning against sin, like "Long Black Train": "Watch out, Brother, for that long black train. . . It sounds so good, but I must stay away. . .don't go riding on that long black train."

Four boys made up the second group. The oldest, Caymon Reynolds, eighteen, played the mandolin. The youngest was his brother Hayne Reynolds, fourteen, on banjo. Ethan Welsh played guitar, and Josh Argo, sixteen, the fiddle. The band's sound was brash and youthful, but they could also render the softer melodies. A capella they harmonized on "Amazing Grace" and sang an original gospel song by Caymon: "There ain't nothing gonna come between me and God, we're like two peas in a pod, me and God."

The group entertained the crowd with old favorites like "The Night They Drove Old Dixie Down" "Salty Dog," and "The Eighth of January." They also sang some "new bluegrass" that included lines like "I'm just here to ride this train, it don't matter where it's going," and "The interstate's the stream where I live, got these wheels in motion and there ain't no way to turn this around." Josh Arno sang one of his own songs, then dedicated a blue collar lament, "Poor Boy Working Blues," to "anybody who has looked forward to a weekend."

The last band of the evening was Browngrass, so called I gathered, because some of its principals were named Brown. Following upon the boys' energy, Browngrass took the evening to a quieter place. By the time the musicians said goodnight, their audience was in a mellow mood. They remarked to one another how good it all was as they folded up their lawn chairs and slowly left the darkened square.

The Orgy Years....

Crime is part of the Gainesboro and Jackson County world, but typically it's pretty dull stuff. The arrest reports published in the weekly Jackson County *Sentinel* are an endless list of arrests for probation violations, revoked drivers' licenses, driving under the influence, banned substances, and worthless checks. Occasionally an arrest for something like "especially aggravated kidnapping" causes a reader to pause and wonder. The same reports indicate that domestic assault is not uncommon.

The *Sentinel* also faithfully reports on local officials charged with crimes small and not so small. In August, 2008, County Commissioner Kim Young was arrested for theft of some $7,000 from the Travelers Insurance Company. Young was the second commissioner arrested within three weeks— Commissioner James Evins' arrest on a DUI charge was also front-page news.

Drug busts, of course, make the paper. A recent top of the page headline, "Meth Lab Discovered on Shady Lane," points up at a contrast between current shady business and a nostalgic vision of summer afternoons in a little town.

But the kind of scandal that gripped the Jackson County sheriff's office beginning in 2006—riveting, eye-popping scandal unfolding month after month—that's unusual. From December 2006 to August 2008 an online chat room devoted to the scandal drew a total of 3,167 posts, which took up 159 pages. On July 25, 2008, a writer happily summed the whole thing up: "We will never forget," she enthused, "the orgy years!!!!"

The *Sentinel* reported in December 2006 that Sheriff Kenneth Bean had asked the county district attorney's office to investigate improprieties in his—the sheriff's—office. Bean, a large, overweight man with close-cropped grey hair, a small mustache, and blue eyes set in a round, full face, denied knowing anything of these improprieties until after his election to a second term in August. The county DA turned the matter over to the Tennessee Bureau of Investigation.

Eventually TBI agents arrived in Gainesboro. Sheriff Bean had alleged that the jailor, Robert Bean, and two women inmates left the jail headed for the inmate garden to pick vegetables but wound up instead at the jailor's house. Sheriff Bean said he wasn't "sure what all happened, but I think I know." The jailor, referred to in news reports as a distant relative of the sheriff, broke under questioning and resigned. "He didn't want to cause any trouble or anything," the sheriff explained.

Another employee, Deputy Jimmy Davidson faced scrutiny for having borrowed $500 from an inmate and for allowing two male prisoners into a cell with four or five female prisoners. According to Sheriff Bean, two of the women admitted this to be true, although no record of the event was available, as the camera in the cell had for some reason something draped over it. Davidson also resigned.

Another action considered an impropriety occurred when jail administrator Lisa Banks gave a Mary Kay party at her house, and two women inmates and a deputy who delivered some tables hung around for the party. Bean said Banks had been reprimanded.

"I'm ashamed and shocked by all of this," news reports quoted Bean. "I'm not going to cover anything up. I'm not that way. I wish I could have stopped it before it got as big as it has gotten."

Citizens, taxpayers, voters, officials of all kinds, politicians, parents and their children, all know the meaning of a cover-up. It is perhaps a primal impulse to hide the thing that if discovered will—at best—make us lesser persons in our own and in the world's estimation, or—at worst—bring that world crashing down upon us. Ever since Watergate, an elected official's denial of a cover-up has become a red flag. Citizens wonder what he/she really has on his/her mind? They have learned to steel themselves—for what they're not yet sure.

In calling for an investigation of alleged improprieties among his staff, followed by reprimands and resignations, Sheriff Bean may have hoped to direct the outcome of the investigation. However, in May 2007, after what the TBI described as a "rather lengthy investigation," a Jackson County grand jury indicted Sheriff Kenneth Bean on thirteen counts of official misconduct, two counts of sexual contact with an inmate, and three counts of sexual battery. According to the TBI, the misconduct began in 2005 and involved ten female inmates. Also indicted were Cynthia Head, a deputy, and office employees Jimmy Stafford, James Draper, and Jimmy Davidson, each charged with various counts of misconduct. All were arrested in late June.

"I'm still saying I'm not guilty," said the sheriff as he was booked into his own jail; " . . . we got to go to court."

It addition to his other problems, Bean, married and the father of five, was separated from his wife, the result of an admitted affair with a now pregnant deputy.

The official indictment said Bean's alleged actions were "against the peace and dignity of the state of Tennessee."

ONE GAINESBORO RESIDENT I spoke to said the arrest ought to have been the end of Bean's tenure. Resignation was surely in order, and what about future female inmates? Could they be safe? But he did not resign, and the vindicating court date kept receding. The first trial date, set for November 2007, had to be postponed when the judge assigned to the case recused himself. Bean said this was suspicious. The next date, set for April 2008, had to be abandoned when the second judge assigned protested he had already set his retirement date. He seemed to have a justified concern. After all, with eighteen separate counts, innumerable witnesses, and various legal maneuvers, the case might take months to resolve.

A new judge and a fall trial date were announced.

By spring, however, consternation in at least some parts

of the community had spread to the point that the county commissioners apparently felt obliged to step into the fray and consider ousting the sheriff. The commission gave no public notice of its impending vote, however. At its April 7th meeting members went into executive session. When the meeting resumed twenty-four minutes later, the vote was ten for the ouster, seven against, and one abstention.

Since no public notice had been given of the ouster vote, Bean's lawyer Jackie Bellar would later describe the executive session as "star chamber tactics throwing a dark and ominous specter over the name of good and lawful government."

In mid-May County Attorney William Draper and Alan Poindexter, a second attorney hired by the commissioners, filed the ouster lawsuit. Poindexter said that Bean's conduct "shocks the conscience of reasonable men." How it affected the consciences of the seven who voted to retain Sheriff Bean he did not say, but the vote of the seven indicates that in Jackson County, family history and connections run deep. Moreover, Bean's success in combatting local drug trafficking had gained him community support. Some felt the word of women picked up for alleged prostitution and drug abuse was being taken over that of the sheriff.

Financial support for Bean's legal expenses came in terms of community fund raisers. County commissioner Willard Mayberry helped organize gatherings in the Center Grove community. Advertised events for a June fund raiser included a raffle, a pot luck supper, and a cake walk. Lue Stephenson, also an organizer, reported she had pledges for some six hundred cakes. She herself had twenty-two cakes already made and stored in her freezer. An added attraction was to be a "Dunk the Deputy" booth, assuming a deputy could be found to participate.

County commission meetings reflected ongoing dissension. In the May 21st edition of the *Sentinel*, Pamela Walton, the correspondent following the story, wrote that recent Jackson County Commission meetings had been "anything but boring" as "sparks flew" between County Mayor Charlie Hix and Willard Mayberry over line-item expenditures submitted by Sheriff Bean. Mayberry accused Hix of "nitpicking it to death," contending that "other departments had padded their line items," which Hix denied.

Property taxes became part of the discord when Property Assessor Kim Hammock confronted the commission over property tax increases. In response, Hix asked, "How are we going to pay all these lawsuits and raises on the same money?" Belinda Ward articulated another point of view, urging that the county pay for Bean's attorneys as it was paying for the county's extra attorney. And what, the commissioners were asked, was the purpose of the ouster, as Bean's trial was coming up? Walton reported that Bean supporters applauded Wishard's remarks several times. The commissioners, apparently uninterested in hearing more of the same, adjourned the meeting even as others waited to speak.

In early June, the first step in the ouster, called a suspension hearing, got underway in the county courthouse. "Public interest was high in the community" reported Walton.

Then, in a surprise move, Bean's attorney requested a jury trial for the suspension hearing. Questions arose as to precedence of civil or criminal trials and the requirements of gathering three juries—one for the suspension of Bean, another for the ouster proceeding, and another for the criminal case. Judge John Wooten ruled to delay the suspension hearing until after the September 15 criminal trial.

In August, Judge Wooten granted Bean's request that each count in the indictment be tried separately, with no witnesses "overlapping," which might prejudice the jury.

This was perhaps wise. One can almost hear the difficulties a jury might have if all eighteen counts were presented together—twelve jurors sequestered in a little room, becoming angry, making accusations, breaking down—the twenty-first century version of the movie *Twelve Angry Men*, only now it would be *Twelve Angry Men and Women* with appropriate dialog. Imagine the frustration, the possibilities for confusion, the discord.

While the alleged actions took some in the county by surprise and they, therefore, had their doubts, in an important sign of the times among Tennessee's youth, a Jackson County High School student wrote in one of the first internet posts regarding the scandal, "People here at my school have known these things for months."

For many of Sheriff Bean's Christian supporters, however, the alleged actions against Tennessee's peace and dignity required a Christian response. They said things like, "We should not judge others. It is not our right. It is God's right," or "Whoever is without sin, let him cast the first stone."

Most citizens looked upon the scandalous cartoon-like goings on at the sheriff's office with embarrassed condemnation, and while the scandal did have its cartoonish aspects, in fact, it involved actual men and women. Over lunch at the El Rey Azetca Cafe in Gainesboro with *Sentinel* reporter Pamela Walton, who brought her own habanero peppers, I asked Walton how she accounted for it.

"We haven't really had a righteous sheriff for years," said Walton, a pretty blond who came to Gainesboro in the Eighties from Florida when that state was beset by a crime wave. Walton says she was robbed several times; in one incident, the robber actually apologized for the intrusion, saying, "Sorry, I'm in the wrong apartment." In another, she was robbed and held hostage at gun point for twelve hours. She sought peace and quiet in Gainesboro.

Mostly she got what she sought, and says until a few years ago people didn't lock their doors or their cars, though that's changed, with drugs mostly to blame. "It's idleness," says Walton. "There are no jobs." For the young there's dealing. Heroin is available, but favored are prescription drugs like Oxycontin. "Older guys on disability get a prescription filled, then sell the pills at forty dollars a pop."

Bean, family man and Christian, ran for office as one who would be that righteous sheriff. Walton says over time he definitely made an impact on drug trafficking, thereby gaining the trust of the community. When rumors began to

circulate about sexual shenanigans at the sheriff's office, supporters considered them an attempt by drug dealers to force
him out of office. Walton says initially she thought that might
be possible, but sources in the DA's office told her, "You can't
believe what's going on over there." When she read the grand
jury's eighteen-count indictment containing the testimony of
ten women, she says, "There were so many of them."

Was Bean ever righteous? Or did he just fail to recognize his weakness and prepare defenses against it? Walton
thinks he was seduced by power and opportunity. "There's
just so much poverty here," she says. A few women, often
young, rootless, and without resources, wind up in the county
jail, and sometimes for a man, "suddenly it may be an opportunity previously unimagined, something beyond his wildest
dreams."

However, Kenneth Bean, Tennessee county sheriff, is
not alone with his problem. In fact, every year the Vanderbilt
University Comprehensive Assessment Program in Nashville
accepts referrals of seventy individuals from licensing boards,
courts, or employers. Ninety percent of the referrals are men
sent to the program because of their involvement in cases of
sexual harassment or abuse. Those referred to the program
come from across the country; they include doctors, CEOs,
lawyers, teachers, and clergy—men, in other words, with
money, education, and position.

Ginger Manley, Clinical Professor of Nursing and Associate in Psychiatry at Vanderbilt and part of the evaluation
team, says there is a "surge people get from any kind of power."

In some cases, the men have already lost what she calls "their moral compass," and use sexual encounters to satisfy a range of desires. For some, power confers a sense of entitlement, stated and unstated, to certain benefits.

According to Manley, now, as always, sex retains its function as a commodity, and sometimes the trade is explicit, sometimes implied. One former inmate's account of her experience in Sheriff Bean's jail indicates how upfront the exchange there was. The woman said, "Well, he took me into his office one morning and had five to six Xanaxes in a sealed thing, and he shook them at me and looked down at his privates, insinuating that he wanted me to do a favor for those Xanaxes." She said she refused; she also alleged that Bean had let the women inmates know he could shorten their jail time in return for sexual favors.

SEEKING REACTION FROM Gainesboro women, I asked several of them what they thought about Bean. One woman told me she believes women in the area don't get much respect, and she feels women arrested and taken to jail may not be safe. Another woman said she thinks family connections and loyalties allow some corruption to be excused or overlooked. On the other hand, one long-time resident told me, "If a woman behaves like a lady, she will be treated like a lady." She believes it unlikely that female inmates would fall into the "lady" category and more likely would be prostitutes or druggies.

However, some women were held on lesser charges.

According to a news report, one woman arrested for driving on a suspended license said she was initially searched for weapons and drugs and locked up. A few days later "the sheriff had her brought to his office and asked if she had a recording device under her clothing. The former inmate said she told the sheriff she had been searched just two days earlier when she came into the jail. Regardless, the Gainesboro woman claimed the sheriff pulled up her blouse and bra and checked her out." She also alleged that he tried to kiss her.

I had planned to spend some time in Gainesboro covering the trial, and I'd be lying if I said I thought it wouldn't be interesting. On the other hand, I could certainly see why most Gainesboro and Jackson County residents hoped the whole horrible mess would just disappear—which in fact is pretty much what did happen.

On the day of Bean's arrest, one news report told of a former inmate rejoicing: "I think it's great. I think he ought to go to the pen for the rest of his life." Some thought he would get jail time.

It was not to be. On Wednesday, September 3, Bean, beset by rising legal bills, pled guilty to two counts of Simple Assault, which is a Class A misdemeanor. In a closed courtroom, he was sentenced to eleven months, twenty-one days, for each count, to run consecutively, and both were suspended. The sentence called for unsupervised probation for two years and payment of court fees and fines. He was not to work as a paid or unpaid employee for any government agency in the 15th Judicial District for two years nor run for public office for six years. He still faced sexual harassment suits in federal court.

So, no jail time, no time in the pen. Just the never-to-be-forgotten orgy years, which actually may have added more than one newcomer to the county. Rumor has it they are known as Beanie babies.

I. Glenn Jones: It Will Happen

If idleness is the Devil's workshop, then it's certain that Glenn Jones is a rare visitor. He quit a job on a factory assembly line in Cookeville where he had worked for eleven years to take up the task of caring for his father, who was stricken with Alzheimer's disease in 2002. After his father's death, Jones, having noticed that he lived in an age of extravagant weddings, set about transforming his home in the rolling hills just south of Gainesboro into a scenic wedding site. Once completed it was to offer a bride and groom and their guests a white, steepled wedding chapel, a reception hall, and formal gardens.

Then one afternoon in July 2004, Jones drove into Gainesboro for a dental appointment. When he arrived, he was told to come back in two hours, because, he said, the dentist was drunk. He does not soften this description with terms like "slightly inebriated," or "three sheets to the wind," or "not well" (wink, wink, nod, nod), but just "drunk."

To pass the time he walked to the Jackson County courthouse and went down into the basement. There he again took up his search for the records of a 1922 trial involving the murder of Jones's great uncle Johnny Cooper, still a young man when he and his best friend visited a bordello in the hills north of Gainesboro. There his best friend shot him in a quarrel over a woman. Jones had searched for the trial records for several years, but on this visit he realized that the records not only were in disarray, but left unprotected by those he described as the "responsible people," they were being looted. "Anyone," he said, "could go down there and take whatever they wanted."*

His realization that the court documents could simply vanish sent him that very evening to the Jackson County Historical Society's monthly meeting held as usual in the county museum just a block off the square.

It seems likely that most of the members of the Jackson County Historical Society did not know Jones. If they had, his experience with some of the members might have turned out differently, for hometown roots can make a difference in the Upper Cumberland. Jones, born in Detroit, was fourteen when his parents left there and returned to Baxter, a town just south of Gainesboro in Putnam County.

He received his high school diploma in Baxter and took some courses at Tennessee Tech in Cookeville but didn't get a degree. He worked as a tour guide in the Center Hill Dam

---

* The lead story in the July 15th, 2009, edition of the Jackson County *Sentinel* was headlined "Lost 1800 Records Are Returned." Local residents had found court records dating from 1841 to 1850 in a box they bought in a nearby county and brought them back to Jackson County. The article reminds readers that possession or sale of county records by a private person is against the law.

power house, then was hired at Gold Metal Furniture in Baxter, where over time he became the shipping, receiving and inventory supervisor. That was the job where he learned how to organize sheets of paper, but after he'd worked there eleven years, Gold Metal moved to Mississippi. He then found the factory assembly line work in Cookeville, so through the years his connections to Gainesboro were limited.

When he arrived at the Historical Society meeting he found the members in a lengthy discussion about the preservation of a pie safe. "I told them, everybody's only concerned about that pie safe, and I pointed at it, when the real history is in the Jackson County Courthouse records, and they're being stolen and carried off as we sit here, and nobody's doing anything about it."

Thus called to action the Society formed a preservation committee to investigate the basement, which it did on July 14, 2004. That day, as secretary for the preservation committee Katherine Anderson recorded in the official log, the committee found thousands of loose court papers, some dating as far back as 1813. Some were simply scattered about, others had no particular order. As the basement had no heating or cooling, mold had damaged the big 19th century court ledgers. "It is totally inappropriate," she wrote, "to continue storing these priceless historical documents in these damp conditions."

A few days later Jones and Historical Society volunteers Larry Mabry, Faye Wilmore, Katherine Anderson, June Vanhooser, and Daniel Poston began the great cleanup. They first moved the records into the driest spot in the biggest vault in the basement, then into another vault. Jones provided locks and chains to keep the records locked in the vaults. This was an acceptable thing to do, he told the other volunteers, until a public records commission could be established.

The volunteers decided that the safest place for the documents was on the top floor of the courthouse, up three flights of narrow stairs from the basement. The area had to be cleaned and a place made for the ledgers, books, and papers. Jones bought carpeting, which he and Daniel installed. Library tables, chairs, wooden card catalogs, shelves, file cabinets, a computer and a typewriter, much of it donated, were installed on the third floor. Volunteers lugged boxes loaded with documents up the stairs, then sorted and labeled the documents.

By September the new public records commission had held its first meeting and elected Jones its chairperson. Members visited the State Library and Archives in Nashville. Jones worked on a cataloging method and went to seminars for archivists. He learned how to index the hundreds of pages of loose records. The commission applied for a $5,000 grant from the State Archives and got it in December 2005. It also asked county mayor Charlie Hix to bring Jones's name before the Jackson County commissioners, who assented to his appointment as the Jackson County archivist. Jones says he didn't want to do it, but, "The main thing is, I knew it needed to be done and nobody else was going to do it." No pay accompanied the appointment.

By 2006 Jones was having conversations with people

from places like California and Texas who came to Gainesboro to search for family records. I was there one October afternoon when two Texas women came and, as they searched, bantered with Jones in a good natured way. One said to the other, "Were you rude to him on the phone?"

"No, I wasn't rude on the phone, I just said some rude things when I got off the phone. He just thinks he knows everything."

Jones, tall, slender, brown-eyed, looking like thirties but actually nearer late forties, baseball cap on, (without the cap he combs his dark brown hair forward, giving him a faintly Napoleonic appearance) smiled a faint, resigned smile and said, "I can assure you I don't know everything." He didn't add the word "but"; however, clearly he stood firm in his belief that he did know pretty much everything about what was in the third floor rooms and how what was there ought to be used. It helped when the two women found their documents, long full pages written in 1871 in the flowery, spidery script of the pre-typewriter age. "Look at this," said one, as she pointed out the signatures of family members at the bottom of a page. She was thrilled and Jones was pleased, vindicated for the moment in his efforts to preserve a piece of county and family history.

As the months turned into years, some of the luster of being the Jackson County archivist dimmed. When people like the Texas researchers wanted to use the archives, Jones had to meet them at the courthouse, unlock the back door if necessary, lead them upstairs and unlock the door to the file room.

Since the researchers couldn't be left unsupervised, he had to sit in the small, cramped rooms and watch them read their papers. "Sometimes," he said, "it takes forever."

Sometimes he would drive to the courthouse and wait around for a researcher who didn't show up. "That's frustrating when you're not paid," he said. "I can't really afford to do this. No telling where this would go if I was actually paid to be here." He was still working on his wedding venue, and said sometimes he wished he hadn't become so involved in the archiving and instead concentrated on finishing his wedding chapel.

For every person like Jones, a man in motion, swept up in the momentum of what he's doing and bent on action, there are those whose inclination is to throw on the brakes. What's all this about? they ask. Who says the records were inappropriately stored? Are all his cards on the table? How much is this thing going to cost? Is this a way to live off the taxpayers? Or, some people asked, is it some kind of power grab?

Jones thought some of this concern stemmed from his lack of Gainesboro roots, in contrast, for example, to John Fox, Gainesboro's mayor, a long-time resident and president of the Jackson County Historical Society. He floated a plan to have the Fox School (named after his father but now empty) remodeled and made into a multipurpose building. It would house the archives, the Historical Society, the county library, the Upper Cumberland Veterans Hall* and community meet-

---

*See "Honoring the Veterans"

ing rooms. That seemed like a reasonable plan, but apparently even Fox was having trouble moving it forward. When at a Historical Society meeting I asked him about his plan, he said carefully, "I thought this was settled, but it turned out it was not."

Jones said, "That building is a fire trap. Would you put invaluable historical documents in a fire trap? Would you put all your historical eggs in one basket? With a volunteer fire department, as big as that building is, everything would be burned up."

As to a power grab, he said, "Well, what's that all about? I am the archivist. I already have the power." Besides, he had his own plans for a new building, and he told me, "It will happen."

II. Glenn Jones: It Will Happen

It was the summer of 2008 when I saw in the Jackson County *Sentinel* that there was to be a Public Records Commission meeting in August, and that the Commission was in search of a new Jackson County archivist. I knew that Glenn Jones had become the archivist for Putnam County, whose county seat is Cookeville, twenty miles east of Gainesboro and the area's big town. Jones told me about the new job when I'd seen him at Jackson County's annual Poke Sallet Festival in May. He had opened the west courthouse door and put out a sidewalk sign letting people know the Veterans Hall* on the third floor was open. "I don't have to come down here and do this," he said in his matter-of-fact way, "but I feel this is a service the community needs."

His new position, he told me, actually paid him a full-time salary *and* provided benefits *and* gave him the opportunity to establish a Veterans Hall in Putnam County.

Even though the Jackson County Archive was essentially his creation, he had been but one of a group of volunteers. Some of the others were longtime members of the Jackson County Historical Society and had their own ideas about how to establish and maintain the archives. Resistance to his leadership apparently developed and grew, then grew some more. On the other hand, in Putnam County he arrived with

---

*See "Honoring the Veterans"

his credibility intact—hired as an experienced archivist knowing what to do and how to do it.

Knowing this background, I wondered what the meeting of the Public Records Commission had in store.

Commission members began to gather in a second-floor courthouse room shortly before four o'clock. There I met for the first time Dutch Warren, given name Ruth, a dark-eyed, slender women who, I learned that afternoon, had served three two-year terms as Gainesboro's mayor in the late Nineties and into the new century. At eighty, she maintained an animated, open, talkative way about her, and I looked forward to asking her for an interview.

As we sat waiting for the meeting to begin, the other attendees and I listened with pleasure to her story. She gestured often with her hands that were still strong and shapely. She said she was born in Jackson County only because her mother came back to *her* mother's house in Gainesboro for each "lying in," but the family lived in Grosse Point, Michigan. She became Dutch because as a little girl she looked exactly like the blond child with the page boy haircut on cans of Dutch Boy paint. She attended the University of Michigan, then became a stewardess for a major airline at a time, she said, "when it actually meant something." Eventually she became a recruiter for United Airlines, and her work took her to every major city in the U.S. One of the commission members recalled Dutch as having that "stewardess look," and wherever she appeared, men took notice.

Just about then, Bill Draper, county attorney and the

commission's secretary, arrived, with Jones following a short time later. After Draper read the minutes of the last meeting, I began to understand that this was not to be a congenial gathering.

Dutch Warren immediately questioned Jones's presence. "You can't serve two masters at once," she said, an assertion she forcefully repeated throughout the hour-long meeting. Then began a contentious discussion regarding the meeting held in April. At that time, Jones had already taken the Putnam County job. When the April meeting opened, Jones was not present, and some in the group took this as indication that he no longer served as Jackson County's archivist. However, it turned out Jones was merely late and had no intention of resigning. At the August meeting apparently the issue remained unresolved. Warren and some other commission members persisted in their assertions that the April meeting ended Jones's tenure as archivist. Jones denied it: he hadn't resigned and would be the archivist until someone else was approved by the county commission.

The Warren faction insisted that Draper had agreed that Jones was no longer the archivist, eventually asking him to poll the members present: Did Draper or did he not say in April that Jones was no longer the archivist?

During all this, Draper, slender, white-haired, dressed in a white shirt, chinos and loafers, mostly kept his head bent over his minutes, but though expressionless, his face with its high cheek bones and wide mouth tensed, and his blue eyes stared more and more frequently into space. Eventually he apparently felt required to review April's events: he recounted that at four in the afternoon he had said he didn't know if Jones was coming as he hadn't heard from him. However, when Jones did show up ten minutes later, no final decisions were made. Now, said Draper, "That should be the end of it."

To which Warren said to Jones, "You can't serve two masters at one time." Jones replied, "I haven't resigned. I'm willing to help out any way I can. I just want it to be done right."

Jones may—or may not—have been Jackson County's archivist when he arrived at the August meeting, but by the end of it, he definitely was not. It turned out an applicant, a woman, silent like me throughout the meeting, sought the job. She was hired on the spot, pending county commission approval. The tension subsided but not the contentiousness. There was an exchange over grants and grant money. An argument arose over the purchase of file cabinets. Jones suggested that the new file cabinets match those already in place on the third floor. Warren rejected this suggestion immediately. Who cared whether they matched or not? It was price, not appearance, that counted.

The upshot of the meeting was that an apparently long-brewing aim of some commission members to oust Jones was achieved. The justification for its success seemed based not on any failure of his as an archivist. It was a personal matter. It was *Jones* that they so obviously wanted gone, and on their own terms—no hanging around being helpful and giving people instructions. Near the end of the meeting it was mentioned that three Historical Society members would go to Nashville in the fall to take the archivist training.

When the meeting broke up, I approached Dutch about an interview. Had there been any hope for success, that afternoon would not see it. "No," she said. "Absolutely not. I don't give interviews."

Outside the courthouse, I asked some others who had been at the meeting what they thought, and someone said, "Well, Glenn has a short temper, and the ladies have put in a lot of work, many hours of work, and when he comes along, for example, and tells them to remove the staples from documents and use paper clips instead, they don't like it."

However, whatever animosity had developed between Jones and other members of the commission, clearly the creation of the Archives and the Upper Cumberland Veterans Hall had been the focus of his bountiful energy and enthusiasm not for mere months but for several years. His time and effort had been eventually rewarded—mainly, of course, by the Putnam County job. Articles about the Jackson County Archives and the Hall had appeared in state historical publications, the Jackson County *Sentinel,* and the Cookeville *Herald-Citizen.* In the area, he'd become well known and had defenders as well as detractors.

Although his success brought new possibilities, clearly he didn't want to sever his ties to Jackson County's archives. But severed they were. Months later he told me he hadn't even been allowed to remain a member of the Public Records Commission. "Do you feel bad about it?" I asked. "No," he said "not at all. They couldn't mold me. That's what they hated. Plus, I found a mess in the courthouse basement and turned it into something. They had decades to save those documents and they didn't do it. They couldn't stand that either."

It isn't unusual for long-time leaders to see the success of a younger, brash, full-steam-ahead challenger as an affront. Still, Dutch Warren, representing a generation near the end of its time, and Glenn Jones, representing a generation ready to lead, might have been collaborators—two energetic, strong-minded, willing workers in the community solidifying gains and creating new possibilities. Glenn could have built upon her energy, seen her as a source of well-earned knowledge. Dutch could have seen him as the next step, someone endowed with new vision, strength and spirit. Instead, they became antagonists, no reconciliation desired or sought.

Honoring the Veterans

Glenn Jones believes in and relies on maps and signs, identifiable points in what would otherwise be a vacant landscape. A map attests to what's real and what's there—or was once there. Signs serve the same purpose, and so during the time that he set up the Archives, he put up signs along Highway 56 to identify where communities once were. On the way north to Celina there's a sign for Old Columbus, a village established where Roaring River meets the Cumberland. Its sign says it was destroyed by Union troops in 1864. There's

Glenn Jones with a volunteer at the opening of the Veterans Hall in Gainesboro

a sign for Meigsville, notable because in the early part of the nineteenth century, along with Sparta and Gainesboro, it was a stop on a post road. Now there's only a bridge over Sugar Creek. To the south there's a sign for Mayfield, a community also lost to

91

time. "You wouldn't know those places were there," Jones said, "if it weren't for those signs."

True, and people would have much less access to Jackson County's court documents were it not for the Archives, and they especially would know less about the area's veterans had Jones not created the Upper Cumberland Veterans Hall. Although both the Archives and the Veterans Hall were initially housed on the third floor of the Jackson County Courthouse, Jones distinguished between the two. The Archives preserve histories found in court documents, he said, "good and bad, marriages to murder," while the Veterans Hall preserves the history of local families, making visible, tangible connections, a map showing Upper Cumberland people living now their connections to the past.

The remodeling of the third floor of the Jackson County Courthouse where the court documents and research materials were to be kept left a hall and a large room empty. The area needed something remarkable to draw visitors up the stairs. Not a veteran himself, the idea of hanging pictures of veterans on the bare walls of the hall came to Jones when he saw television coverage of soldiers returning from Iraq and realized that most Jackson County residents knew very little about their fellow citizens serving in that Middle East war. Then he thought, "What about Viet Nam?"

He began to talk about his idea with others. Ballard's Art & Frame in Cookeville agreed to frame photographs of soldiers for families who provided an 8X10 photo, information to identify each soldier, and twenty dollars. Veterans and families took up Ballard's offer, and the Upper Cumberland Veterans Hall was dedicated on February 4, 2005. The first picture hung that day was of Fred A. Ballard, killed June 7, 1944, during the Normandy landing.

Soon the hall was filled floor to ceiling with photos of veterans and those killed in combat. Most were from World War II, no doubt because the manpower required for that war was so huge in proportion to the nation's other wars. The Gold Star photos of those killed in that war occupied the center section.

With the framed photos Jones included places and dates of birth and death (if available) and the battles some survived and some did not. In addition to the photo on the wall, he provided a manila folder with a second photo. Sometimes the folder contained only the photo, but sometimes families added newspaper clippings, commendations, family genealogy, and other tokens.

That was just the beginning. Over time visitors to the Upper Cumberland Veterans Hall could see in the empty room documents and paintings starting with the War of 1812, the one that made Andrew Jackson a national hero when he and his small army of Americans defeated the British at the Battle of New Orleans in 1815.

Jones filled the room with rows of wooden cases with glass doors he built to display plastic models dressed in service uniforms. Some cases displayed Union and Rebel uniforms and memorabilia from the Civil War. Veterans and the families of whose who died in the nation's more recent conflicts donated uniforms, fatigues, boots, snapshots, and mementos meant to bring to mind the familiar passages of American life.

It had always been obvious that the third floor of the courthouse could not be the permanent location for the Archives or the Veterans Hall. Some residents couldn't make the climb up the stairs ("You gotta work to get up here, doncha," was the usual remark of those who could and stopped to take a breath upon their arrival.) However, getting them moved took some five years and considerable conflict and struggle. Initially Jones favored an empty city-owned lot and a new building. In a fund-raising drive thousands were collected, but the project stalled.

Maybe fate had a hand in it, for in time a new path opened up. Jackson County's jail had maintained for years what could politely be called a certain medieval ambience. The upstairs—small, dark, cramped, with rusty, moldy shower stalls provided for male and female inmates and prisoners squeezed together in tiny, dank cells—presented a perfect scene for a gothic "this is the South you've always imagined" movie. The sheriff and his family lived downstairs. Finally in 2008 the state of Tennessee demanded the jail be moved to a building suitable for the incarceration of living beings. The closed county hospital became the jail, leaving the old building empty.

"It's perfect," said Jones. One of his earliest requirements was that the court documents be archived in a safe location, and the jail was perfect because "It's a vault. It's fire proof." In his plan the upstairs would provide a safe repository for the Archives and the downstairs an accessible home for the Upper Cumberland Veterans Hall. The money already raised would help pay for the remodeling.

.   Committees came to look over the building. Supporters could already see walls and plumbing torn out, bathrooms, partitions and windows added. Doubters saw a money pit. Could there be enough dollars, they asked, to make the old jail a place where people would actually want to sit down at a table and peruse court documents? As to locating the Veterans Hall downstairs, who knew what it might cost to fix up that mess?

Jones remained ready to press on with the renovation. "It will happen," he said.

On July 15, 2009, the Jackson County *Sentinel* featured a group photo of nine jail inmates in stripped trousers and shirts, one holding their award certificate for demolishing concrete walls, tearing out drywall and studs and removing old plumbing at what the *Sentinel* called "the historic" old jail. On July 29th the paper reported that the renovation continued, aided by a group of young people hired through the federal stimulus program. The paper quoted archivist Susie Cummings saying, "It was dirty, gritty work during some of our hottest days." By August the renovation was almost complete.

The Jackson County Archives and Upper Cumberland Veterans Hall on Short Street opened to the public on Veterans Day, November 11, 2009, followed by an open house the following Sunday. A large, appreciative crowd came to the now modern public building painted a brick red with white trim. They toured the Archives rooms upstairs, hosted by members of the Public Records Commission, then went downstairs to spend time looking at exhibits and more than four hundred photographs of area veterans and those lost at war. Jones, arriving at the open house in the middle of the afternoon, was greeted warmly downstairs by supporters serving as hosts.

"A visionary," they said, "that's what he is, he's a visionary."

The Veterans Hall in Putnam County

By 2008 four years had passed since Glenn Jones walked into the basement of the Jackson County Courthouse in search of the court record of a 1920s murder. What he saw in the basement—masses of court documents unorganized and subject to decay and pilfering—turned his life in a new direction. The documents needed to be saved, and he would save them.

When I first began writing about his experience as an archivist in Jackson County and saw the interest and intensity he brought to the work, I thought perhaps he saw this kind of preservation as his "calling," that thing in life he was meant to do, but when I asked him if he thought so, he looked at me quizzically and said, "No, not at all." Then I wondered if the veterans halls he assembled first in Gainesboro and then in Cookeville represented a central direction for his life. Again he denied any particular sentiment. "I put my heart into everything I do," he said. "I do the best I can." He added that the historical work he'd most enjoyed over the last five years had been putting up signs along local highways identifying locations of long forgotten towns.

However helpful those signs may be, they clearly don't connect Upper Cumberland people to their past in the same direct way the veterans halls do. Area residents recognized the value of the Putnam County Veterans Hall almost immediately, and in the first few months, they brought in more than four hundred framed veterans photos.

Jones's own family connection is to Putnam County. While most of his forbears were Confederates, one great, great uncle joined the Rebel forces in 1861, then switched sides after two years. Making the change required that Captain Prettyman Jones — Prettyman being his mother's maiden name — be denied the option of resigning his CSA commission. Instead, he had to desert, then go to Kentucky to enlist in the Union Army, in which he also became a captain. After the war he returned to Putnam County, and Jones said his name is on the cornerstone of the Putnam County Courthouse. Born in July of 1841, he died in July of 1917, the year the United States entered World War I.

Sometimes the personal information provided with the photo ushers in a mystery. Major Zina G. Mitchell, Sr., for example, survived the Philippine Insurrection and WWI; then, the note says, while a member of the National Guard, he was "killed by a fellow soldier" at the Calvary Barn in 1936. Was it passion, money, regulations?

With the framed photographs, Jones includes places and dates of birth and death (if available) and the battles some survived and some did not. It is this bit of battle information that takes a visitor beyond local remembrance into the nation's military history. For example, CSA volunteer Hiram Martin, Tennessee Infantry Company, served from 1861-65 and was wounded at Shiloh, Millsprings, Murfreesboro, Tullahoma, and Corinth. During World War I, local men saw service in the

Argonne Forest, the massive and final Allied offensive which ended the war. Some photos are of Great War soldiers who made it home but died from the effects of poison gas. Serving in Korea from 1951-53, Corporal Cooper Allen saw action at Death Valley, Heartbreak Ridge, Punchbowl, and Porkchop Hill.

Just as in Jackson County, most of the photos are of those who served in World War II, and the photos, the battles, and the casualties suffered demonstrate what is meant by the term "world war." Putnam County in rural Tennessee saw 108 of its soldiers killed. Photos of some of the them hang in the Veterans Hall, but as Jones said, "There will never be 108 pictures. People move away or die, so there's no one to keep up the history of their family."

The battles took local men to Asia, Africa, and Europe and provide a general time line of the war's progress. In the Pacific theatre, battles in which Putnam County men fought included the Philippines, Luzon, the Solomon Islands, the Marshall Islands, New Guinea, Iwo Jima, and Okinawa. Some served in China and in the occupation of Japan. Some survived the Africa campaign, and like Alfred Clark, went on to follow the war in Europe through Italy, France, and Germany. Some made it through D-Day, then became POW's. Some trudged through Europe with Patton's Third Army. Some died in the Ardennes Forest in the Battle of the Bulge in the winter of 1944-45, just a few months before the April end of the war in Europe.

Like the Upper Cumberland Veterans Hall, the Putnam

County Veterans Hall provides visitors with a look at families who sent three, four, five, or six sons to serve in WWII. One family sent six sons and all came home. Another Putnam County family lost a son in November of 1944, and he was buried in the Philippines. His younger brother, killed thirty-three days later, was buried in England. One family sent five sons, and all came home but one. Grateful they must have been, but how they must have mourned the one lost.

There are photos of soldiers who served in Korea and Vietnam and a Marine who survived the 1983 barracks bombing in Beruit, Lebanon. Then there was Bosnia, the first Iraq war, and now Iraq and Afghanistan.

In January, 2007, U.S. Army Ranger Ronald Johnson died in Iraq. In April of that year, Eric VanAlten, 82nd Airborne, was killed in Afghanistan. Then in September, Lance Corporal Lance Clark died in Iraq during his second tour of duty. VanAlten and Clark were twenty-two years old. The showcases their families provided hold their dress uniforms, fatigues, boots, commendations, formal studio photographs, and snapshots taken in the field. Vivid snapshots of milestones in the life of the young — graduations, proms, sweethearts, friends, and family — make them seem still at home in the world.

Visitors wander up and down the narrow aisles, looking at these Americans in their uniforms, their faces unlined, their eyes the eyes of the very young. There are a few officers, but most of them are the equivalent of the G.I.'s of WWII. Women are rare, almost none until Vietnam, when photos show a few local women who enlisted and served as nurses.

There are no photos of African Americans or Native Americans. When I asked about this, Jones reminded me that there have been virtually no African Americans in Jackson County or Putnam County for decades—the 2007 census update estimate is .9 percent in Jackson County. The 2007 census update for Putnam County estimates two percent African Americans out of a population 71,000. American Indian population in Jackson County is .3 percent, the same as Putnam County. Jones says one African-American father whose three sons served the country visited the Putnam County Hall and discussed bringing in photographs, but no pictures arrived.

According to the note with his photo, Paul Franklin Davis, a U.S. Army soldier serving from 1961-64, "aided Federal troops enrolling James Meredith" at the University of Mississippi in 1962.

His note reminds me that in our country there are many histories.

Memorial Saturday

Just as the Methodist Church bell rang noon, I parked my Honda under a tree big enough to shade half the street and part of a small playground. Concerned I might be late, I hurried down the street—literally, as Gainesboro is built in the hills—toward a line of motorcycles that blocked off the west side of the square.

Turning the corner, I eased into a spot in the narrow strip of shade the buildings facing the south side of the courthouse offered. I glanced down the street and saw nearly everyone had squeezed up next to a building or stood in a doorway. The crowd was large enough to show the organizers of this Memorial observance that their efforts were not going unnoticed.

Around me stood people who knew one another. Several men stopped to warmly greet and shake hands with a man to my right. In front of me was a young woman, very trim in jeans and a colorful shirt, noticeably upright and with an independent air—possibly military at some point, her hair now in a spikey cut. Next to her stood a tall, lanky, red-haired man with a long face and a damaged left forearm. When she turned her head to look at him, I saw her profile had the same neat look as the rest of her. They seemed easy together and respectful of one another; I thought they might be father and daughter. Visiting briefly with the man others had greeted, he said, "Yes, we bitched all spring about the cold and now we'll bitch that it's too hot."

The cycles, it turned out, belonged to a Rolling Thunder contingent of ten or so bikers on their way to Washington for the annual Memorial Day service on Monday. They milled around, talked with Jackson County Sheriff's deputies, and looked official in black trousers and black leather vests. One good looking man, ruddy faced, well built, and with a full shock of white hair, had various decals sewed on the back of his vest, including on the left-hand corner the infamous "Jane Fonda, Traitor," and under Traitor, BITCH.

Across the street, ceremony participants also milled around, waiting their turn at the wooden podium placed on the sidewalk leading up to the courthouse door. A stunted tree provided them some sparse shade. Straight down the street, just over midway down the block, several rows of steel folding chairs sat empty in the sun.

After fifteen minutes or so, the Master of Ceremonies, who sounded like a minister, got the program going. His opening prayer was longish, covering all the bases—the day, the veterans, the participants, the audience, Rolling Thunder, thanks for, then request for, God's help. A soprano began "The Star Spangled Banner" a capella. When her name was announced, someone down the line said, "Yes, she does a good job with it," recognition that the rendering of the national anthem by a lone singer creates tension. This tension increases as the singer moves inexorably toward "the free"—the most likely place where something unpleasant could happen. All went well, however, and I thought I could feel a sigh of collective relief when "of the brave" faded.

We joined in the Pledge. Before I moved to Tennessee I never thought much about the "under God" phrase, but the Buckle of the Bible Belt has got my back up a bit, so I now have decided to stand on principle and omit "under God." I'm rejecting this contentious prepositional phrase because it was added to the pledge in the mid-Fifties by what I consider McCarthy types. However, a man among the program participants, another minister, I supposed, boomed out "under God," so we were like the proverbial couple casting our opposing votes. Had it come to an actual vote, I was well aware that I was in the minority.

Then began the recitation of poems. An elderly woman whose speech had a strong Tennessee flavor and who was dressed as Uncle Sam gave "That Ragged Old Flag." Someone recited "In Flanders Fields." This poem caused me to remember the red paper poppies veterans' organizations used to sell on Armistice Day. In my mind I heard the words of a World War I song that begins, "There's a long, long trail a winding into the land of my dreams, where the nightingales are singing and a pale moon beams."

105

Mrs. Lois Goggins, the English and music teacher at my country school in New Mexico, had the choir sing that and other World War I songs on special occasions. That was in the Fifties, too, when there were still those who took part in the passions WWI stirred and remembered its eleventh hour armistice. Today it's most often considered so great a waste of life and resources, and its consequences so disastrous, as to be almost inexplicable.

At about this point in the program a tall blonde woman rose to the microphone and asked, "Is It Decoration Day or Memorial Day?" She explained how Memorial Day wasn't actually a national holiday until President Lyndon Johnson suggested it in 1968 and Congress approved the change in 1971. She concluded with "and that's how it happened." She sounded pretty combative, which made me wonder if she suspected there were those in the crowd who might, in spite of all evidence to the contrary, insist on saying "Decoration Day."

The Master of Ceremonies then called the veterans by war to their special chairs in the sun. A few from The Good War remained, some frail or in wheelchairs, and a few from Korea, but most were from the Vietnam era. When the Vietnam vets were called, the tall, lanky man in front of me glanced at the young woman beside him as if to ask, "Should I go?" She smiled at him and gave his shoulder a little push. "Yes, go on," she urged, "go on." His face cleared, and he walked down the street to join the others.

When all were seated, the emcee said, "I count between forty and fifty veterans." Everyone clapped, and I thought that was quite a few veterans for a small community.

Speeches from elected officials followed. I was thinking the vets in the sun might like to get this over with when a stocky, round-faced man in a brown suit and tie reached over and took the mike from the emcee, who lowered his head and looked displeased but resigned. It was the "under God" voice; he spoke for a while, mentioning again those "who made the supreme sacrifice" and stressing "under God." This time a murmur of assent went through the crowd.

Finally the emcee reclaimed the mike and announced the color guard. They marched into the street and stood at attention. The crowd was asked to recognize each service as the sound system provided the stirring marching songs — "The Shores of Montezuma," "Those Caissons Go Rolling Along," "Anchors Away." The Marines got the most applause. I clapped most for the Army; somewhere in me the U.S. Army still represents the ideal of the citizen soldier.

From about this point I lost track of the order of events. Eventually the emcee released the veterans; the lanky man came back grinning and said, "Well, that's that." There was a rifle salute. For the first time I saw down by the veterans' chairs two small, old-time cannon. Two men loaded and fired them three times. When the booms stopped echoing off the hills, Taps was sounded. The notes were so clear and firm I looked around for the bugler, then realized the mournful notes emanated from the sound system. I'm not saying this was bad; these days sometimes its easier to find a soprano than turn up a bugler.

Somewhere near the end the emcee introduced a Rolling Thunder spokesman. He described the group's mission. It acts on behalf of veterans, he said, then provided a long list of the failures—the sins of omission and commission—of the U.S. government in its treatment of the nation's veterans. At times like this I have to wonder how much daylight there is in a democracy between that democracy's citizens and their government.

A woman wearing a well-fitting blue suit with white trim, white hat and white pumps, read the last poem, and the soprano sang "The Lord's Prayer": "Forgive us our trespasses as we forgive those who trespass against us." The man sporting the Jane Fonda decal bowed his head along with the rest of us sinners.

In truth, there is no end to irony (little and big) in human life and history, but think too much about that and you'll wind up misanthropic or solitary, a wanderer in the desert—or, as someone suggested to me, maybe a comedian. So, I was happy to let it go and head for the City Cafe on the corner down by the cannons. There in air-conditioned comfort I had two big glasses of sweet tea and a good hamburger.

When I stepped back out into the bright, hot light, the square had emptied. I walked back up the street past the courthouse just in time to see Rolling Thunder mount up and head for Washington. A slender boy, ten or eleven maybe, rushed up from the opposite direction. We met in the middle of the street and watched the bikers bank into a left turn, hang there on the edge for just an instant, then rev their engines and disappear.

We looked at one another. "Boy!" he exclaimed, delighted, his blue eyes wide. "They make a noise, don't they!"

Southwest

We see the world once, in childhood;
the rest is memory.

> Louise Glück,
> Meadowlands

Before the Town

Thirteen hundred miles west of Gainesboro, Tennessee, and a few miles west of the Texas-New Mexico state line on Interstate 40, are the remnants of a town: a few gas stations, a few houses, a school, and some empty brick buildings. Interstate 40 travelers zip past, but if they looked south they'd see what people who put up roadside markers call a place of historical interest. Local people call it the Caprock.

The Caprock escarpment rises hundreds of feet into the sky from the flat plain. Riding east on horseback in 1541 the Spanish conquistador and gold seeker Francisco Coronado saw the cliffs of the escarpment. Behind him to the northwest were what he had thought would be the gold-filled cities of Cibola. The "cities" turned out to be in large part earthen dwellings of Native American tribes in Arizona and New Mexico. Now, leading an army, he was headed toward Quivera, another land a trusted guide convinced him was filled with gold. (He later had the guide strangled.)

When Coronado saw the steep cliffs of the Caprock, he called the area the *Llano Estacado,* translated for generations as the *Staked Plain.* Somehow the word *staked* caught people's imagination, conveyed the mystery and danger of the empty, trackless, grass-covered, treeless land, flat and vast as an ocean. However, the preferred translation now is the *Palisaded Plain*, which retains the idea of the cliffs as Coronado the soldier saw them—a defense similar to the palisaded or staked enclosures the Spanish built to protect their settlements from Indian attack. Over time the *Llano Estacado* came to designate an area of more than 37,000 square miles in eastern New Mexico and west Texas. Its northern boundary is the Canadian River, and it was on the banks of that river, twenty miles north of the Caprock, that newcomers established the village of Logan near the turn of the twentieth century.

The Llano, remote and rarely even seen by white people as late as the 1870s, was a very small part of a vast empire the Spaniards called the *Comancheria*. They did not go there, and in effect ceded to the Stone Age, nomadic Comanches large parts of what is now eastern New Mexico, west Texas, the Texas and Oklahoma panhandles, the Wichita Mountains in southwestern Oklahoma, half of Colorado and Kansas, and parts of northern Mexico.

The Comanches arrived in the Southern Plains around the beginning of the 18th century. They were originally of the Shoshones in Wyoming, but as the tribe became a horse culture, some migrated south in search of pasture land. The Ute tribe of southern Colorado gave this group their name, which means *enemy* or *foreigner*. In 1706 with the Utes they visited a trade fair the Spaniards held in Taos, New Mexico, their first encounter with Europeans. Over the next few decades, they

114

added to their skill as archers an unmatched skill in horsemanship, skills they honed in war. They became everyone's enemy, and by 1730 the Comanches had driven the once powerful Apaches out of northeastern New Mexico and areas farther east. Like the Apaches, the Utes, Pawnees, Arapahoes, Kiowa, Tonkawa and any others eventually had to accept Comanche domination of the Southern Plains.

In his book published in 2010, *Empire of the Summer Moon*, subtitled "Quanah Parker and the Rise and Fall of the Comanches, the Most Powerful Indian Tribe in American History," S. C. Gwynne writes that the Comanches patrolled their empire and "ruthlessly" enforced its boundaries. Anyone who entered the Comancheria without their permission risked a tortured end. Their domination, according to Gwynne, had been secured "with extreme violence, and that violence had changed their culture forever." The Comanches "quickly evolved, like the ancient Spartans, into a society entirely organized around war, in which tribal status would be conveyed exclusively by prowess in battle, which in turn was invariably measured in scalps, captives, and captured horses."

They captured horses and cattle in battle but were also notorious horse and cattle thieves. They used the stolen livestock to supply other tribes and eventually white settlers, then sometimes stole them back. They raided Mexico for slaves, wives, horses and mules. By the late 1830s, when the Cherokee and other tribes in the American south were forced west to Oklahoma, the Comanche raids into Mexico became so disruptive that Mexican states like Sonora, Durango, and Chihuahua offered a four-dollar bounty for an Indian scalp. The Comanches continued their raids even after the 1846-48 Mexican-American War treaty required the U.S. to stop them, and during the California Gold Rush they raided Mexico to steal horses for the hordes heading for the gold fields.

With the vast buffalo herds of the plains guaranteeing an unending supply of meat and hides, Comanche population increased to more than 20,000, which was augmented by women and children captured in raids on other tribes and later on white settlers. The children* were typically well treated and raised as a part of the tribe, but the treatment of captive women, Indian or white, was brutal in the extreme.

Gwynne estimates that they were at the peak of their power in the mid 1840s, raiding and killing at will, but by 1855 decline set in. Diseases such as smallpox, measles, whooping cough, and influenza thinned the population. The great cholera epidemic of 1849 that swept the frontier decimated

---

*The most famous white captive was Cynthia Ann Parker, known everywhere on the frontier as the White Squaw, seized as a child and raised as a Comanche. She became the wife of a Comanche chief and had two sons; when she had the opportunity to return to the white world in 1846, she chose to remain with her husband and sons, the oldest of whom was the Quanah of Gwynne's title. In 1860 in a skirmish with the U.S. calvary, her husband was killed. Their two boys escaped, but she was returned to the white world with her toddler daughter, Prairie Flower. In despair she sought for years to find a way back to her sons and the Comanches. Instead, she wound up in the deep woods of east Texas, far from the open plains. Her daughter died of influenza in 1864, and Cynthia Ann died of influenza and possibly self-starvation in 1870.

Indian tribes all across the plains. By 1867, the 20,000 had dropped to probably fewer than 10,000, and would continue dropping. The epidemics took not only lives but a sense of cohesion, of being able to understand the world. No Comanche medicine man could contain or explain the deaths, especially from cholera, which could kill in a day.

What was clear to the tribe, however, was the meaning of the buffalo men.

A new tanning method made the buffalo hides valuable, and a railroad line in Dodge City, Kansas, took them to the eastern markets. Using powerful rifles the buffalo men could kill hundreds of the big, lumbering animals in a single day—a lucrative day's work, since each hide brought $3.50. They hired men to do the dirty job of skinning them; the carcasses were left to rot. Gwynne writes that between 1868 and 1881, the buffalo men killed thirty-one million buffalo, the biggest kill in human history. It was partly for money, partly "a final solution" to the Indian problem. In Gwynne's description, they "stripped the plains" of the animals that were at the core of the hunting and gathering Comanche life.

An attempt by an independent Comanche band to stop the destruction of the buffalo resulted in the Buffalo War and Red River War of 1874-75. The attempt was unsuccessful, and the defeated Comanches were herded to a reservation at Lawton, Oklahoma. Gwynne writes that the war, actually more of an antiguerrilla campaign, had about it "a grand finality." It was—at last—the last frontier. "You could see it, grasp it: the end of the horse tribes' dominion was the end of

117

the very idea of limitlessness, the end of the old America of the imagination and the beginning of the new West that could be measured and divided and subdivided and tamed first by the cattlemen and then by everybody else. Within a few years barbed wire would stretch the length and breadth of the plains."

The displacement of one group of people by another is one of humanity's oldest stories, but few displacements have been so complete or so final as that of the native peoples from the Southern Plains. The Comanches had drifted at will across the Plains, living without written history, clocks, or calendars, their lives guided by their horses and wars, the migrations of the buffalo, and the changing seasons.

It's as if you entered a theatre to watch a play. An act ends, the curtain drops and when it rises again, the walls of the Llano Estacado are still there, but the cast of characters, in terms of how they look and dress and speak, how they eat and live, how they think and what they value, bears no resemblance to those you've just seen. Those now on stage know almost nothing of the original inhabitants. They are the new world. On their stage the transforming sound is the whistle and roar of the railroad steam locomotive. Waiting in the wings are washing machines, automobiles, airplanes, a vast array of new technologies, and, in that mechanized world, wars more lethal than the Comanches could have, perhaps, ever imagined.

Village Merchant

Homesteaders in eastern New Mexico at the turn of the 20th century arrived after any threat of Comanche attack was at least thirty years past. Spanish landowners offered some resistance, as did the cattle barons, who hated to see their free, fenceless prairie turned into minuscule 160-acre plots. Sometimes they hired gunslingers to run off the settlers, who told stories of houses burned, or sometimes just hauled off, and crops destroyed.

Four decades earlier Abraham Lincoln had issued the Emancipation Proclamation and the Homestead Act on January 1, 1863.* The newcomers to the Llano Estacado were laying claim to some of the last of the free land, and they were not to be deterred. They looked at the waist-high grass on the virgin prairie and called it a paradise.

---

* The act was signed in May, 1862. Opposition to free land was especially strong among southern slave holders, so it was not until the South seceded that the Act could get congressional approval. The act ended three decades of agitation by reform groups and eastern laborers that began in earnest with the financial panic of 1837 and the resulting low wages and unemployment. Later panics (1857, 1873, 1893, 1907, 1929) also forced displaced people west.

Some came to New Mexico territory by wagon, but by around 1900 settlers could arrive by railroad boxcar, their belongings, including livestock, ready to be unloaded at a railroad water tower somewhere on the prairie.* The Rock Island Railroad, which originated in Chicago before the Civil War, established the first railroad stop in what is now northeastern New Mexico in 1901 at Nara Visa, just a few miles from the Texas border. Twenty miles farther west railroads brought in workers to build a railroad bridge across the Canadian River to open rail traffic from Liberal, Kansas, all the way to El Paso, Texas. Just north of the bridge construction site a tent village on Howry Ranch land housed the workers.

The site seemed promising, with its depot and a bridge about to be finished, and some people thought that just being close to a river in that part of the country had to be a good thing. True, the river (its headwaters in the foothills of the Rocky Mountains near Raton) was usually just a few pools reflecting sun and sky in a wide white river bed, but several times a year tons of water suddenly roared by in a single day. The site's possibilities led railroad engineer Eugene Logan and J. E. Johnston to purchase the land the tent village occupied for $400 and lay out a town in the typical grid. Initially, east and

---

*Between 1863 and 1934, 1.6 million American citizens or those who had applied for citizenship filed on a 160-acre plot for a small fee. If homesteaders "improved" a portion of the 160 acres over five years it became theirs. After one year the land could be bought for $1.25 an acre. About three quarters of the land went to industry and speculators.

west streets had Spanish names—Gallegos,* Martinez, Armijo, Garcia, Vigil, and Fuentes, indicating a strong Spanish influence. North and south streets were First, Second, Third, Fourth, and Fifth.

Why Logan's name was given to the new settlement is unknown, as are the details of his life. Perhaps he was the prime mover, or perhaps it was a cut of the cards in the Morales Saloon and dance hall. By way of contrast, in Tennessee in 1817, Gainesboro's founders in Jackson County named their town to commemorate General Edmund P. Gaines, noted for his part in military actions against Florida's Seminole Indians and in the War of 1812. By 1901—thirteen hundred miles west and almost a hundred years later—the past the Tennesseans honored seemed long ago and far away.

It turned out that Logan's promising future came and went pretty quickly. By the middle of the 1950s when most of the United States enjoyed post-World War II abundance, the

---

* When the anglo homesteaders arrived in the Logan area, they found a Spanish community. Gallegos, twenty-five miles north of Logan, was the site of a large Spanish land grant ranch founded by the Gallegos family in 1870. It provided its own currency, mounted patrol, and community services, including a Catholic church and priest. Petra Gallegos of Clayton served as Logan's first school teacher. She taught one month in Logan, one in Gallegos, and one in Bryantine, a community northwest of Logan. The second teacher was Elatorio Baca, the third W.W. Moore. One of Logan's first school board members was N. Martinez.

The Spanish-speaking residents were uniformly Catholic; the newcomers were uniformly Protestant and brought with them the prevailing Protestant predilections. Long before I knew the town in the 1950s the Spanish-speaking residents had been marginalized.

Plains were beset once again by drought and bone dry for most of the decade. Those who survived the Great Depression and the Dust Bowl, then enjoyed the prosperity engendered by the war, once again faced natural disaster. As Logan became a windblown collection of dusty streets, some moved on, some hung on. I was a Logan High School student, and my parents, L. O. and Mable White, hung on to a small ranch south of town.

By the time I knew the town in the 1950s I didn't think of the streets as having names. Rural homes got their mail delivered via a rural route, but Logan residents picked up their mail at the post office. People just knew where other people lived. The street we called Main was the site of the McFarland Brothers bank, the Osborn Brothers Garage, the U.S. Post Office, Fitzner's grocery store, the People's Drug, the Clark building, Mrs. Cromer's grocery, Opal Lee's Beauty Shop, and Shollenbarger's Hardware and Lumber Yard. To the north of Main the Anglo part of town had some graveled and some paved streets and houses with fenced yards and lawns. To the south in the Mexican part of town brown, hard-packed dirt roads marked by bone-jarring potholes ran past small adobe and rock houses.

On the east side of Logan, Highway 54, originating in Chicago and paralleling the railroad tracks, produced a steady stream of traffic. West of Highway 54 at the corner of Main street and the original Third Street stood three two-story buildings and one large abandoned building of brown sandstone. It had for that little town a striking doorway. Above the door-

The door of the brown sandstone building adorned with the Shollenbarger name. *Photo by Matalina Smith*

way were two arches, the first framing what apparently had been a large curved window and anchoring a ram's head. On each stone of the second arch was one letter of the name Shollenbarger—obviously the reason for such a big arch. The lowest stone on each side of the arch rested on three fluted columns with carvings on their tops and pedestals ending in stone tree roots. The columns framed what had been a large double door set so that it invited shoppers in from three directions. When I became aware of the building, the doorway and all its windows were blocked by heavy corrugated tin.

Across Main street from the vacant sandstone stood a long, rectangular, stuccoed, two-story building—Shollenbarger's Hardware and Lumber Yard, which took up most of the block. On the lower level two plate glass windows faced Main and a row of plate glass windows looked out on Third Street, all with green and orange stripped canvas awnings. The upper level sported rows of large double windows. The lumber yard occupied the north end, and on north across the street was the two-story brown sandstone school building surrounded by elm trees.

Catty-cornered across from the sandstone was the D. W. Clark Building, its large plate glass windows facing Main. What had been a dry goods business was closed, but through the windows its darkened interior was faintly visible. It appeared as though one day someone simply turned off the lights in the Clark building, leaving what merchandise remained to gather dust. I was surprised when I heard that someone lived upstairs, for I never saw a soul.

Across the street was Dr. M. M. Thompson's two-story, with its plate glass windows. In a small slice of the east side of it Doc Thompson maintained a cluttered office lit by a bulb dangling from the high white wooden ceiling. He was rarely seen, becoming, some said, even more reclusive after his younger son Glenn was killed in Germany by a sniper just before the end of World War II. Most of the downstairs was taken up by the People's Drug, with a soda fountain, wooden booths, small round marble tables, and large display cases. In back were shelves and more shelves full of drug store bottles. Harry and Lela Reid and their children Jennie and Bobby lived upstairs in some of the rooms. Other rooms were occasionally rented.

Clearly, these four buildings spoke of another time, but back then I never thought to ask why they existed. In school we studied the Spanish Conquistadores, the northern New Mexico Pueblos and Navajos, the pioneers, and statehood. I knew as much about whatever better times Logan had seen as I knew about the time the Comanches ruled the Llano Estacado, which is to say nothing.

Then, at the end of the 20th century, almost fifty years after I left Logan, I interviewed Joe Shollenbarger, retired and living in Amarillo, Texas. As a teenager I was aware of him and his hardware store because I went to school with his sons Kenneth and Joe. I remembered their father behind the counter of his well-stocked store, a man in his middle years, slender, with noticeable eyebrows, brown hair and eyes, and wearing his carpenter's apron filled with the necessary tools—not unfriendly but all business, reserved, a bit solemn. During a long afternoon's talk, I learned that his father, Joe Hiram, who went by J. H., built the sandstone and the two-story building. I glimpsed what the buildings meant to the Shollenbarger family and the town. I also saw that Joe had kept alive within him the memory of the time when he, his father, his mother Elsie Anne, his brothers and sisters, and Logan itself were young and their futures open.

By 1902 LOGAN HAD A depot with its required railroad water tank, the Burns Mercantile Company, a wagon yard, the bridge workers' tents, and the Morales Saloon, which catered not only to the bridge workers but to cowhands at the Howry ranch, whose headquarters lay several miles to the east. Soon to come were the J. S. Johnston building, the Gallegos building, and McFarland Brothers Dry Goods, which became McFarland Brothers Bank.

The bridge builders finished the first bridge in 1901, then had the pleasure of living in their tents and collecting a paycheck from the Rock Island, Chicago, and Pacific railroads a little longer than anticipated. At four o'clock one morning the first bridge they built swayed, buckled, and collapsed just as the southbound train's caboose reached the far side.* Details are sketchy—no newspaper existed to assign an investigative reporter to the story and expose wrong doing—but the cause was said to be "poor footing."

Seventeen-year-old Elsie Anne Sears heard the collapse.

Elsie Anne, born in Macon, Missouri, in 1884 to Frank and Addie Sears, spent much of her young life on the move. Her father was one of those men, people said, who just couldn't settle down. Maybe he was a man with a romantic nature who wanted to see what life was like in places he'd never seen, or maybe he just kept hearing the call of a new opportunity. Living in Macon, he'd heard of the great wagon trains that once left the town of Independence and headed west on the Oregon Trail. Whatever his reasons, Frank got together enough money to buy two mule teams and a covered wagon, which he drove to Denver. His wife, two sons, and three daughters

---

*However, the engineers got the hang of the thing after their first failure, and finished the second bridge in 1902. Freight trains rumble over the high bridge in the 21st century just as they did over a hundred years ago.

arrived there by train a month or so later, and in the early summer the family set out for Idaho.

From Denver the Sears family could make their way north to Cheyenne, Wyoming, and there pick up the Oregon Trail, which took travelers all the way to Salt Lake City (a route somewhat similar to what is now Interstate 80). Straight north from Salt Lake lay the Snake River, the Snake River Plains and Pocatello, Idaho. Whatever route the family chose led them through some of America's most spectacular scenery, which sometimes made up for how hard it was to travel for months in a covered wagon with two mule teams and five children.

Perhaps the possibility of settling on irrigated farmland drew the family to Idaho, for in the 1880s and '90s Idaho turned to its mighty rivers for hydropower and irrigation. Some who moved to Idaho to develop irrigation projects made great fortunes, but Frank was not one of them. To get the family back to Denver he had to sell one of his mule teams. Broke and discouraged, from Denver they went on to western Oklahoma, an area opened to white settlement in what

---

*The family may have been caught in the financial downturn that was beginning in the early 1890s and turned into a depression (sometimes known as the Long Depression) in 1893. In that panic some 15,000 businesses declared bankruptcy and five hundred banks, many of them in the west, failed. Tight credit, high unemployment, foreclosures ensued — all the usual results of financial crashes. As in the crash of 2008, many people in 1893 had to walk away from newly built homes they couldn't pay for, giving rise to the shiver of dread people came to associate with the empty, "haunted" Victorian house.

had been Indian Territory.*

Joe Hiram Shollenbarger, born in 1875 in Oskaloosa, Iowa, came near to winding up an orphan after his parents separated when he was a year old. He was saved from the possibility of a childhood in an 1876 orphanage by his grandmother Lena Beck, who took the baby with her when she moved to Kansas City. She stayed there for some ten years, then moved with her son and grandson to Boyd in Beaver County in the Oklahoma panhandle, known as No Man's Land until 1890 when Congress opened it to white settlement.

At twelve years old, the boy got a job sweeping out the train depot in Boyd, his first taste of railroad life. When he and his grandmother moved to Kirksville, Missouri, someone gave him a chance for a solid job as an apprentice telegraph operator for the Santa Fe Railroad.* In Kirksville, while he was still a boy, his grandmother took him to the Purcell Studio for a professional photograph. In it his short, straight hair lies close to his well-shaped head; his face, a nice oval with almond-shaped eyes, has an expression serious and contained. His nice three-piece suit with long trousers seems a little loose for his slender form, and a dark bowler-style hat that he holds in his left hand looks like it might be several sizes too large. He's turned slightly

---

*In a period of railroad expansion, then consolidation, the Santa Fe became in 1887 the famous Atchison, Topeka & Santa Fe. Contraction followed expansion, and in the financial panic of 1893 the ATSF, along with the Philadelphia & Reading, the Union Pacific, Northern Pacific, and some seventy other railroads declared bankruptcy.

to the right with his right hand behind his back.

He advanced to telegraph operator over the next decade. Famed for their footloose life, railroad men expected to be on the move, and J. H. had railroad jobs in Kirksville, Pampa, Texas, Woodward, Oklahoma, and Chihuahua, Mexico.

However, by 1898 J. H. must have had enough of rambling, for he took a job in New Mexico Territory as farm foreman at the Howry Ranch, known as the HOW for its cattle brand. Its headquarters were fifteen miles east of what became Logan. He stayed at the HOW for four years.

J. H. Shollenbarger *Photo courtesy Ken Shollenbarger*

In 1902 he was twenty-seven, a man out west living on his own. A photograph from around this time shows him to be of medium height, slender, and wearing a dark suit of some heavy material, probably wool, with the trousers sharply creased and his shoes shined. His hair is full and dark; his oval-shaped face with its regular features and serious eyes has the same contained look it had in the photo made years before. Again, he's turned just slightly away from the camera, right arm behind his back.

He saw eighteen-year-old Elsie Anne Sears for the first time in the middle of September, 1902. What was between them was apparently settled almost immediately, and they met only a few more times before boarding a train in December for Santa Rosa, one hundred miles west. He must have worn his good dark suit and hat. She would have worn her best outfit, perhaps a long full skirt that she paired with a blouse popular at the time called a shirtwaist, which featured a high stiff collar and a ruffle across the bosom. Also fashionable were straw sailor hats decorated with a wide black velvet ribbon.

Did they elope? Was there no minister or justice of the peace in Logan? Or Tucumcari, twenty miles to the south? Did they meet secretly and barely catch the westbound train? As the clacking train wheels took them westward, they must have looked at one another and at the other passengers, gazed out the window across the sea of grass and imagined what was to come. They stepped off the train in Santa Rosa, and a justice of the peace married them the day after Christmas.

Whether they met with approval or resignation on their return to Logan, they were on their way. J. H. quit the HOW Ranch and went to work as a telegraph operator for the Rock Island Line. Over the next two years he and Elsie moved on to other towns and other railroad jobs. In 1904 they came back to Logan where he worked as a blacksmith and then as a driller of water wells. Energetic and ambitious, he'd become a jack-of-all-trades.

They settled in, seeking security and a settled life while

Shollenbarger's General Store, around 1912. *Photo Courtesy Kenneth Shollenbarger*

at the same time open to the possibilities of a new community. By January, 1907, J. H. and Elsie had bought the Galbreth-Foxworth lumber yard. In February they welcomed their first son, Joe. By 1911 they'd sold the lumber yard and began building the sandstone (with a basement) that was soon to become Shollenbarger's General Store offering groceries, hardware, shoes, baked goods, dry goods, feed and coal. By 1912, customers had to be impressed when they walked through the store's double doors topped by the big curved window, two-tier stone archway and the three columns on each side of the door.

The stone had been quarried from somewhere on the Canadian River, but just where has been lost, as have details about the stonemasons, but the stone was well cut, chiseled and sanded. Also unknown is how much J. H. knew of the architectural style of the door, which is called Richardsonian Romanesque, popular in the U.S. in the 1870s and 1880s and named after the architect Henry Hobson Richardson. A guide to American architecture published by the National Trust for Historic Preservation in the United States calls the style "uniquely American." Buildings in this style have a rough texture emphasized by the stone and "by deep window reveals, [and] cavernous door openings." Windows and doors were often defined by "short, robust columns." The guide says local builders across the country used elements of Richardson's work—including broad round arches—for commercial

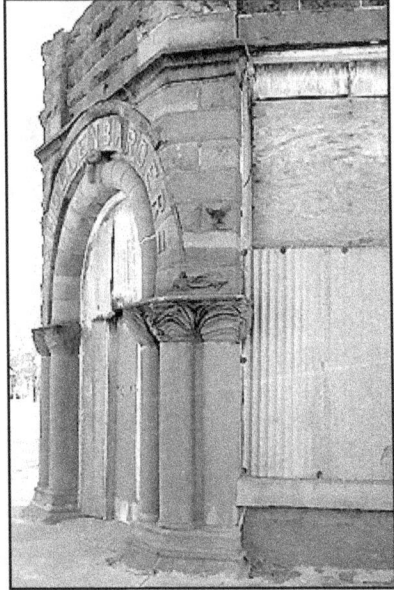

Sandstone columns on each side of doorway of the Shollenbarger building   *Photo by Matalina Smith*

and federal buildings, post offices and schools.

The Shollenbarger building was completed around the time New Mexico celebrated its entry into the Union in 1912 and became the fourth largest state after California, Texas, and New York, a fact school children recited with pride.

By 1912, when the population was a few hundred and the assessed value reported to be $195,000, Logan had considerable building going on. A $1,500 Baptist church built in 1910 welcomed worshipers. The community had passed a $6,500 bond issue in 1910 to build a new school when J.H. and Sim

McFarland of the McFarland Brothers Bank served on the school board. Besides the depot, the land office, the bank, and the Shollenbarger store, the town could count among its businesses a hotel, a print shop, a tin shop, a movie house, and Mrs. Cromer's dry goods and grocery store.

In an age noted for its brotherly organizations, Odd-fellows and Woodmen of the World and their auxiliaries enjoyed one another's company in their halls, and Masons and Eastern Stars met in their Masonic Lodge. The *Logan Leader* newspaper kept up with local gatherings and in 1912 reported that "This vicinity witnessed a scene last Monday that resembled a funeral process, but it was only this [Logan] and Pleasant valley neighborhoods heading toward the sand hills for plums. There were eight wagons and from the amount of people on each," the writer concluded, the plums and the good company must have been plentiful.

By 1916 J. H. and Elsie had become the parents of two other sons, Ray and Benjamin, and a daughter Dorothy. J.H. bought Elsie a washing machine with a mechanized ringer between the two wooden tubs, Logan's first. He drove (and partly built?) one of the town's first automobiles, a Michigan, which ran on an acetylene tank attached to its side. It required a match to light its headlights.

He took up photography, developed and printed photographs of the Michigan and the sandstone building. He documented the construction of the house the couple built in 1916 and lived in for the rest of their lives. The photos show a car in the carport and a windmill, which meant they had a well and didn't

133

have to buy and haul water from someone else's well. Over time he bought more land, served as a director of the McFarland Brothers Bank, built more buildings, started other businesses.

NEWS OF THE UNITED STATES entry into World War I in 1917 came to Logan by telegraph at the train depot and spread quickly among townspeople and area farmers. The Shollenbargers bought Liberty bonds, and as the months passed, J. H., Elsie and the kids joined the rest of the town at the depot to wave their greeting when a troop train passed through, always going south. Behind the depot they could see the camp of the twenty-five soldiers sent to Logan to guard the railroad bridge. Apparently the Huns (or their saboteurs) could be anywhere.

By 1919 when the boys sent overseas came home, J. H. and Elsie undoubtedly heard singer Nora Bayes' recorded version of a song from a Broadway musical which became the hit of the year when it asked:

> **How you gonna keep 'em**
> **down on the farm,**
> **After they've seen Paree?**
> **How ya gonna keep 'em away from Broadway**
> **Jazzin' around and paintin' the town . . .**
> **And who the deuce can parleyvous a cow?**

While many a young man went happily back to the farm, many did not, for the song captured the ferment and excitement the war brought to America. It's a big world out there, said the song, you yourself may want to spend some time jazzin' around. Americans liked the sound of that, and after a short recession following the war, they welcomed the Jazz Age and the Roaring Twenties, one of the biggest expansionary decades in U. S. history.

JUST MONTHS BEFORE ABRAHAM LINCOLN issued the Homestead Act in January of 1863, he signed the Pacific Railroad Act to at last build a transcontinental railroad. Before a major effort could begin, the Civil War had to end, and so it was not until May of 1869 that the famous golden spike linked two railroads, one coming from the east, one from the west, at Promontory Summit just west of Odgen, Utah. This first transcontinental railroad was 3500 miles long. By the end of the century various railroad companies would complete four more — and receive in the process some thirty million acres of free land. Railroad companies built thousands of miles of railroad track, and people in villages like Logan sometimes gathered at the depot just to watch the trains go by.

By the early 1920s, however, the U.S. was already deep in the Age of the Automobile. The country had established the U. S. Bureau of Public Roads in 1918; by 1925 its director, Thomas H. MacDonald, proclaimed in the *Chicago Daily Tribune* that the auto had "dug the U. S. out of the mud." By 1927, 88,000 miles of highway had been built, a drop in the bucket in so vast a country, but a start. Soon, the federal government, state governments, county and city governments would build and maintain roads and highways. In an age when millions could own cars and roads for them were everywhere, the romance of the road took on a new and democratic meaning.

135

Initially, Logan appeared well suited to take advantage of the new age, situated as it was on an "auto trail" known as the A P—the Atlantic Pacific, which ran from New York City to Los Angeles in the early part of the century. Developed and maintained by individuals and private groups, the auto trails aided travelers in what was essentially unmarked territory. Numbers were given to different parts of the trail, and the number 54 was given to that section between Jefferson City, Missouri, that curved into Logan from the northeast and ended about a hundred miles to the southwest at Vaughn, New Mexico, a railroad town on the prairie.

As the U.S. highway system expanded, it replaced the auto trails but retained some of the numbers, including the number 54, which became U.S. Highway 54 out of Chicago. While the history of the building of early federal and state highways in eastern New Mexico is sparse, Logan residents must have considered the possibility that the town could reap the benefits not only of a U.S. Highway 54 but of New Mexico state highway 39, which followed section lines through the valley north of town, eventually making its way into Logan. (See map on page 151.) Or perhaps expectations centered on some old AP route through the village. In any case, Logan's entrepreneurs apparently had some expectation that the highway would run past the Shollenbarger sandstone building.

This expectation produced Logan's one and only building boom. J. H. rented out his sandstone, and across the street he and a partner by 1922 had built a new two-story rock and concrete multi-use structure that took up most of the block. A big plain rectangle, it looked modern and made the sandstone he'd built ten years earlier look definitely 19th century. On the first floor was the hardware/dry goods/lumberyard, and in time a Ford agency selling Model T's, then Model A's and Ford tractors and a garage to keep them serviced and repaired. On the second floor were hotel rooms, a dining room, and the Masonic Lodge, of which he was a member.

He was not alone in acting on the possibilities. Doc Thompson and D. W. Clark built on each of the other two corners the Clark and Thompson buildings, both two stories with businesses downstairs and hotel rooms upstairs. In the three buildings clustered on the three corners there must have been at least thirty hotel rooms. Maybe it was just Roaring Twenties enthusiasm—who could even estimate how much money could be made when Americans took to the road in their cars—but the location appears to invite head-to-head competition. What could each one offer to attract travelers? Clark named his business the Alamo Hotel and advertized it as "the only hotel in Logan with camp ground adjoining."

However, the enthusiasm of the Logan entrepreneurs must have turned into concern. Just as at the turn of the century the Rock Island and the Southern Pacific railroads required a bridge across the Canadian River if they were to continue their expansion, a little over twenty years later a bridge had to be built to accommodate auto traffic. (Until it was built some intrepid travelers motored across the railroad bridge.) It turned out that the new bridge would be built just a few hundred yards west of the railroad bridge. This decision raised questions about the shortest route to the bridge if the federal and the state highways intersected perhaps somewhere north of town.

Planning and construction of the bridge began some-time in 1921. At the chosen location the auto bridge had to be high and long. Crews started on the north and south river banks and kept building un-til the parts met in a high arch.

Logan School students about 1916
Photo courtesy Kenneth Shollenbarger

Those like Elsie who had been around to hear the collapse of the railroad bridge would have hoped *that* didn't happen again, but everybody knew construction meant workers with money, and this time instead of living in tents they would lodge in the Shollenbarger Hotel—or the Alamo Hotel, or the Thompson Hotel.

AS A CHILD J.H. AND ELSIE'S oldest son Joe came to know all the streets in town, its businesses and houses and the people who lived in them. He knew the farmers from the valley to the north who traded at his father's store and knew where in the farming valley they lived.

Like so many others, he answered the call of the river. It was where kids snuck to when they had a package of cigarettes, where lovers went, where church youth groups and end-of-the-year school classes went for hot-dog roasts. The young explored east and west of the railroad bridge, waded in warm, shallow pools on summer afternoons and told one another stories about quicksand, and sometimes stood in quicksand and felt themselves sinking until the moment came when they needed to pull one foot out fast and put it on solid ground. They walked barefoot across the bright, hot sand and saw how each one's footprint was so unexpectedly different.

When a roar that could be heard all over town announced the river had come up, as it often did spring and fall before the advent of upstream dams, he joined townspeople headed for the river bank to watch the water rush down the wide bed. When it had settled some, kids would find a low spot on the river bank, wade into the water and float down to the railroad bridge, then walk back up to their spot and do it again.

He knew all the people who gathered at the railroad station just to watch the trains go by. During WWI he sold Liberty Bonds and joined in the patriotic fervor the crowd felt when they gathered at the depot to greet troop trains heading south. He went to school with the McFarland cousins, Robert and Jamie, and the Fitzner, Osborn, and Meeks brothers and sisters, families that would build their lives in the area.

Joe was attending the two-story school constructed of the same brownish, chiseled sandstone as his father's building. It had a double wooden front door, rows of windows on all sides upstairs and down, and hardwood floors varnished to a high gloss each summer when school was out. He'd toiled

with other grade schoolers downstairs, then in the sixth grade
began to yearn for the seventh grade. Oh, the thrill of going
up the wide stairway that led to the junior high and high
school classrooms, to claim
one's right to sit in the big
study hall and whisper to
a friend at the next desk
and look out through the
high curved windows at
the sky!

During his high
school years he played trum-
pet and cornet in the school

Logan School, around 1912   *Photo*
Courtesy Arelene Wright

marching band and his best friend Jamie McFarland played
saxophone. They were part of an extracurricular group of players called the Sandstorm Syncopaters. In 1925, just at the center of the decade whose aura of prosperity and possibility reached
even hopelessly far-from-anything places like Logan, he was
one of seventeen in Logan's graduating class.

He played baseball, then truly the national pastime, and
pictures of him in uniform show him to be, like his father, of
medium height with dark hair and eyes, strong eyebrows, and
a serious demeanor. He was one of the young men who played
on school teams and also on teams fielded by area communities. Betting on those teams was common and the stakes high.

The bridge builders provided new baseball talent. In
1922 Joe played on what he called Logan's "best baseball team
ever," and the pitcher was one of the bridge men. The team

Logan's 1920s baseball team. Joe and Ray Shollenbarger are standing on the right *.Photo courtesy Kenneth Shollenbarger*

went to a tournament in Tucumcari prepared to take the championship. However, Joe recalled years later with still fresh disdain, "They bought off our pitcher." The Logan boys thought he threw the game to pick up "a wad of cash."

It was baseball and good times and bridge workers bringing the two parts of the bridge together in a rainbow arch. When they finally met, celebrants gathered in the summer of 1922 on one of the tallest* and longest (300 feet) steel arch highway bridges in the southwest. After dedicating speeches were complete, a band commenced to play and the crowd danced on the bridge, which began to vibrate and sway, which, in turn, raised fears that it would collapse—shades of the crash of the railroad bridge twenty years before! Authori-

---

*A new bridge built a mile or so farther west in the 1950s is much lower and straight across—no rainbow arch.

Postcard of auto and train bridges near Logan. *Courtesy Arelene Wright.*

ties cleared the bridge, and years later Joe marveled at the "awful mob scene."

Just wide enough for two cars to pass—riders on the passenger side could reach out and shake hands —the bridge always felt like it was weaving, or shaking, or *something*. As the bridge aged, travelers heard and felt the clack and clatter their car tires made when they hit a repair. People assumed that the bridge would, of course, hold, but a smidgen of anxiety took hold as they found themselves so high up midway across the river.

THE FORD MOTOR COMPANY, after eighteen years of producing the Model T ("You can paint it any color as long as it's black," said Henry) in December of 1927 released its new Model A (available in four colors) with a minimum price of $385. It sported a four-cylinder engine, three-speed manual transmission, and mechanical drum brakes. It got 25-30 mpg.

In 1928 J. H. sent Joe to Denver to become a Model T and Model A certified mechanic at a Ford factory school. He made the return trip to Logan over three days in a new Model A. He may have taken the old Highway 39 into Logan that wound through the valley and into the town, past the Clark, Thompson, and Shollenbarger's hotels.

However, the story of highways in America is a story of winners and losers. U.S. Highway 54 and New Mexico Highway 39 do meet just north of Logan, and clearly the shortest route to the new bridge was not the old Highway 39. The shortest route was a few blocks to the east of the three hotels and the sandstone, missing them not by much, but just enough. When the highways were paved, travelers zipped through the village and headed for Tucumcari twenty miles south, a bigger town with more choices in food and accommodations. Out of sight, Logan's hotels were soon out of mind.

STILL, IN 1928 THE MODEL A was news; people gathered at Shollenbarger's Ford Agency to look under the hood, check the interior, take it for a test drive and maybe buy one. Between December of 1927 and 1932, Ford produced almost five million Model A's ranging from the elementary roadster to the deluxe towncar at $1400. In an age of unbounded optimism, buying a deluxe Model A Ford Roadster seemed to many a car-loving American an achievable dream. By 1932, however, far fewer. On Black Tuesday, October 19, 1929, the Jazz Age, like a record on a player winding down, faded. By the autumn of 1932, a quarter to a third of the American work force was unemployed.

Even before the crash, J.H. had noticed that the farmers on whom much of his business depended struggled as farm commodity prices fell. Logan was in an area considered arid, but rain accompanied the boom years, leading farmers to accept the odd but optimistic notion—a kind of advertising motto that lured them to the Plains—that "rain follows the plow." Credit abounded; farmers could borrow to enlarge their farms and buy farm equipment. Increased production resulted in lower prices, then a bumper wheat crop in 1931 sent wheat prices lower still. As prices fell, farmers, trying to meet their debt obligations, plowed under more and more grassland. In the Llano Estacado, cultivated land doubled between 1900 and 1920 and more than tripled between 1925 and 1930.

In 1932, the U. S. Weather Bureau reported fourteen severe dust storms; in 1933, thirty-eight. On Black Sunday, April 14, 1935, wind took Plains soil all the way to Chicago and dark Plains dust hung in the air in Washington, D. C. In 1937, the Bureau reported 134 severe dust storms, and in the Texas and Oklahoma panhandles and adjacent areas of New Mexico, Colorado, and Kansas, the wind blew away some 850 million tons of Plains topsoil. By 1939 it had also taken away about a quarter of the Plains population (some 2.5 million souls), the largest migration out of an area in a short period in American history.

A song by Jimmie Rodgers, known as the Singing Brakeman and the first country music recording star, stands as a Great Depression lament:
All around the water tank

waitin' for a train. . .
A thousand miles away from home. . .
I walked up to a brakeman
to give him a line of talk
He says if you've got money
I'll see that you don't walk
I haven't got a nickel,
not a penny can I show
He said get off you railroad bum
and slammed the boxcar door.
. . . .
I'm a thousand miles away
from home just waiting for a train.
Oh la-ee, oh la-ee, oh la-ee

AMONG OTHER LOGAN FOUNDERS and area homesteaders, the Shollenbargers held on, and, as always, people knew good times along with the misery of the drought and the depression. One of the good times was the Chicago World's Fair, which opened in May of 1933. Joe and Robert McFarland were determined to go that summer, but a round trip ticket on the Rock Island cost more than they could gather, and, of course, they needed some walking around money when they got to the fair. Over the years they most likely listened to the stories J.H. told of how hoboes hopped freights and evaded railroad detectives, so they decided, in Joe's words, "to hobo it." Their middle-aged fathers, remembering their own days of semi-dangerous youthful adventures, probably saw the trip, as the young men did, as a test and trial of manhood. Their disbelieving mothers imagined the perils and shook their heads in resignation.

It was not an easy ride. From the Tucumcari freight yard, Rock Island freight trains ran through Plains country where the drought was taking hold. In the heat they rode northeast through the Texas and Oklahoma panhandles into Dodge City, then hundreds of hot miles across Kansas and Iowa. From Davenport, Iowa, the line went straight east into Chicago.

For two young men from a village in eastern New Mexico, attendance at the fair, an event so successful it was extended for several years, stood as the adventure of a lifetime. Chicago fair organizers selected technological progress as the theme and named the fair "A Century of Progress" with the motto "Science Finds, Industry Applies, Man Adapts."

In the white buildings in the Moderne style built along Lake Michigan's shoreline, Joe and Robert found the vast Hall of Science, which explained actual scientific processes, famously including how a television set would work when one was actually turned on in a living room twenty years later. The Homes of Tomorrow exhibit showed what new technology meant for home construction and comfort. The fair highlighted modern transportation, and the new streamlined Burlington Zepher actually came to a stop at the fair grounds, having made the trip from Denver in a record breaking thirteen hours and five minutes.

And cars. There were cars enough to hold the imaginations of the car-struck young men for years to come. Displayed in a great domed building was a Nashe, a Pierce Arrow, a Cadillac, a Lincoln-Zepher, and the Best of Show winner, a Packard Special Sport Sedan. Packards were the luxury cars of the time, so long and sleek it seemed only movie stars could match their beauty—Clark Gable had one custom made for him. They were capable of at least ninety miles an hour, but at seventy mph "whisper quiet and highly refined."

Technology may have been the chosen theme, but conflict over social issues, especially race discrimination in a variety of forms, made the news. Complaints arose also when, given the recent ascendancy of Hitler in Germany, the German Graf Zeppelin landed at the fair and stayed for an hour. In addition, in what today would be considered an unsuitable designation, midgets staffed a hall called Midget City.

Far more popular than the science and the home improvements exhibits was the excitement of the carnival midway. Joe and Robert, with their small town, Baptist upbringing, had intimations upon leaving Logan of the temptations they would encounter in Chicago, that toddlin' town notorious for sin and raucous living. Even so, they joined the throngs crowding the carnival midway. In one hall, appreciative crowds followed each swish of Sally Rand's famous fans. Not actually naked behind her fans, she wore a body suit, but some of the righteous found that sufficiently shocking. Maybe Joe and Robert resisted paying their carefully rationed money to see Sally—but, maybe they didn't

They didn't hobo it back to Logan. When they stepped off the passenger train, they were full of accounts of the trip, the fair, and Chicago—some stories for their elders, others for their peers. They perhaps sensed that the Chicago trip might be their last adventure. Robert had planned on getting an engineering degree from New Mexico State University in Las

Cruces, but as the depression deepened and his money ran out, he'd been forced to return to Logan where he worked on a ranch his family owned. Joe moved to Mosquero, a little town fifty miles to the north, where he worked in a family hardware store.

Through the years, J. H. carried his customers on credit annually, which worked in times of a good harvest, but as the depression and the Dust Bowl misery persisted, J.H. sold to people on credit who then found their land worthless and themselves penniless. It was said that he accumulated some land in exchange for debt, but it was also told that he burned several thousand dollars' worth of notes, and some promissory notes worth hundreds of dollars were never collected.

The rain returned in 1941, big, gushing rains all year that washed the dust out of the air and sent water rushing down creeks, windblown gullies, and dirt roads. In the years when dust filled the air, there must have been times when J. H. told himself it was the dust that dimmed his sight, only to slowly recognize that it was *him*, that the darkness was *in him*. In 1940, he had some sight, but by 1943 he was totally blind.

He had been part of a time and a place where his innate creativity, his openness to experience and his business sense served him well despite some personal struggles. His success and Logan's growth linked the two for some thirty years. True, all did not end as he'd hoped. He and others in the community had built for a future they believed to be on the horizon, only to see their biggest plans pushed aside by circumstance and change far beyond what they could anticipate or control.

Able to hear the rain, breathe in the smell of rain in a dry country, the scenes he could see were all memory: his grandmother's worn hands, himself as a thin boy in a suit holding a hat in his hand. The train depot in Chihuahua. Seeing Elsie in September that first time. The deep satisfaction of bringing up a well pipe filled with water. Their children. And so often, the sandstone building with its wide front door framed on each side by three columns.

Dorothy, Ben, and Ray found lives beyond Logan. In Mosquero Joe was thirty when he sold Helen Goats a green watermelon. Not the best way to begin a relationship, but they got past it and married in 1937, with their two sons, Kenneth and Joe, arriving within a few years. Joe bought out the Logan business in 1942 and moved back to Logan with his family. They kept the business just over a decade, then sold it and moved to Colorado Springs where the two boys finished high school. For Joe, however, home was not anywhere he hung his hat—it was Logan. He and Helen returned to the village and built a motel and restaurant on Highway 54. He was glad to get back, he said, "to where I knew everybody."

.   Unlike his friend Robert, his companion on their trip to the World's Fair whose life would be broken, (see "A Demonstration to the Authorities") Joe's life, like that of most people, was blessed by a continuity that befits human experience. Although his father's death came in 1947, his mother lived until 1974. He knew the roller coaster of courtship and marriage, the joys and responsibilities of being a husband and a father, the satisfaction of business success. No doubt he also knew

149

sufficient failure, disappointment, and sadness along the way, but his marriage endured, his sons successfully took up law and accounting and provided daughters-in-law and grandchildren. He retired comfortably with his mind clear and his body able.

When the Logan community began in the 1970s holding school reunions in the high school gym, he attended almost every hot July, delighted to gather once again with those who had shared his youth. He lived to see the rush of Canadian River water dammed and Ute Lake formed. The lake brought in vacationers and retirees and new businesses along the highway. Boosters advertise Logan as "Best Little Town by a Dam Site."

He also lived to see his father's big two story building torn down. Where it stood is now empty space, as is much of Main street. The building made from sandstone quarried somewhere on the Canadian River still claims its corner.

Remembering when, section line by section line

The farmers in the valley to the north of Logan provided most of the Shollenbargers' customers through the years. When I interviewed Joe Shollenbarger in 1999, he gave me a map of the valley and the people who lived there around 1920. As is often the case in these matters, however, when some longtime Logan residents saw the map, they felt changes needed to be made. They met and redid the map.

The lines represent section lines. The names show the land owned by the first filers or those who owned the land about 1920, and the location of their homes. The dark line to the left shows the original Highway 39. Its route explains the location of Logan's three hotels, marooned when the current Highway 39 was built. Arelene Wright brought the group together, and Jim Payne provided the map. Raymond Walker, Junior Osborn, Janet Bradshaw, and the Barker sisters—Coe Beverly, Peewee Porter, and Rue Simon—helped add the names. Their interest preserves part of Logan's history.

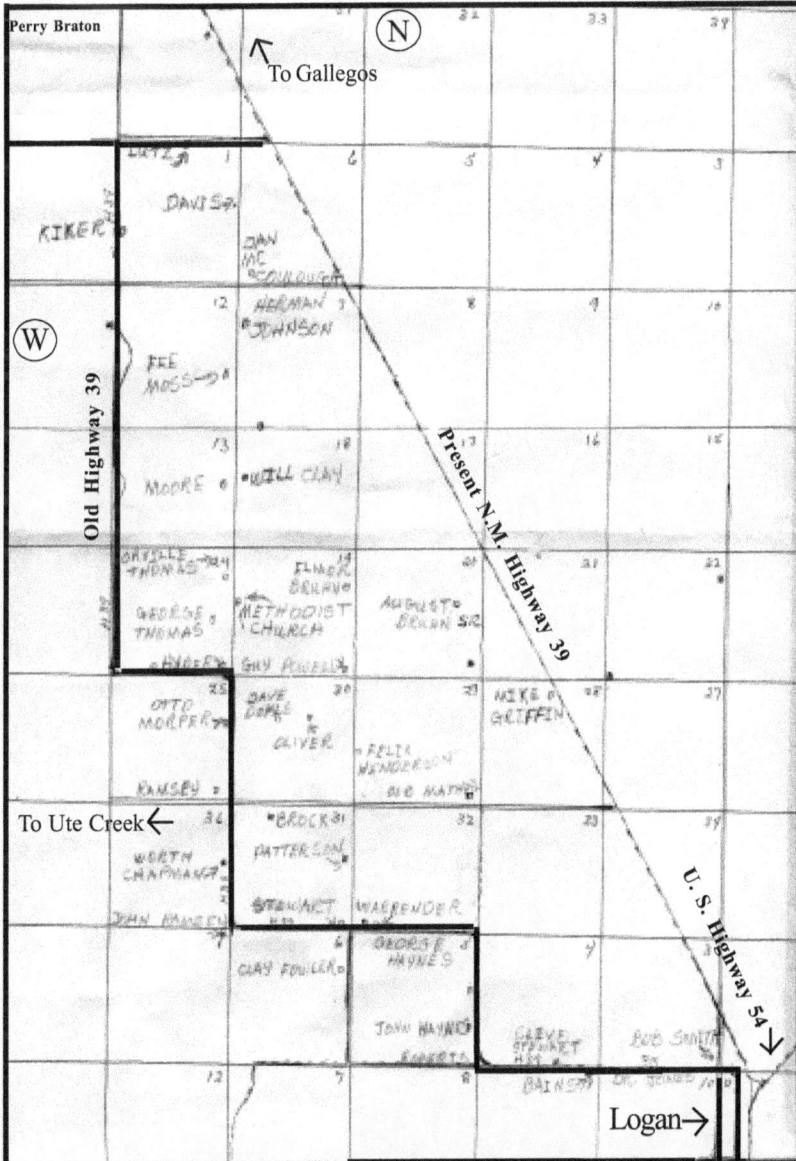

A Demonstration
to the Authorities

In the fall of 1961 the leaves of the cottonwood tree in front of the McFarland Brothers Bank on Logan's Main street blazed gold under a cloudless southwestern sky. The long Fifties drought had passed into dry-country lore. JFK was in the White House and the 1960s prosperity was on its way. In story and pictures, magazines like *Life* and *Look* explored the wondrous possibilities of the coming new technological age. The country read and marveled.

McFarland Brothers Bank, established 1904 *Photo by Matalina Smith*

I was a young woman then, married, and a college student in far away Louisiana. I returned that fall to visit my parents and enjoy a few of New Mexico's autumn days. It seemed the country would move into a golden time. As it turned out, however, the photo spreads in *Life* and *Look* couldn't prepare us for what was on the way. In a few short years, the country would find itself in the midst of experiences that would ennoble some, diminish some, and destroy others.

The bank of rough brown sandstone was a block west of Highway 54. Two plate glass windows, one with the bank's name scripted in black lettering, took up most of the front of the shotgun style building. Inside, Robert McFarland and his wife Ovene worked shoulder to shoulder with his father, Sim McFarland, who with his brother Fred had established it in 1904. The bank stood steady through the Great Depression, the Dust Bowl, World War II, and the Plains drought of the 1950s. To the extent people in the community consciously thought about the bank and its place among them, it was probably to assume that McFarland Brothers Bank, solid, reputable, would continue its role as the financial center of the community. It would always be there. One reason it would always be there was Robert and Ovene's only son Bobby, who in the early 1960s was away at the University of New Mexico in Albuquerque. He was to carry on.

As I remember them, Ovene and Robert were a noticeable pair. She was almost as tall as her husband, and he was over six feet. Both were big-boned, heavy set, and slow moving. Both seemed to me to keep their large, dour faces expressionless, but that may have been just my child's view of them. She had a longish face and sharp grey eyes. Robert's most attractive feature was his large blue eyes framed by thick lashes, but they were partially masked by small wire-rimmed glasses. He had about him a reserve born of his Scottish ancestry, his Baptist upbringing, and his banker's responsibilities.

But there was perhaps more to his reserve than I knew

at that time. When he was a young man, he had apparently struggled to succeed on his own. In a brief history of the family he wrote some time after 1982, he recalls that after graduating from high school he worked for four years, then enrolled as an engineering student at New Mexico State University in 1930, just as the Great Depression settled in. Two years later he left the university to search for a job. When he didn't find one, he returned to Logan to help with his family's ranch just north of town, but even that ended badly, when, he wrote, "Drought and depressed market prices forced the final liquidation of the cattle business in 1934."

That was also the year he and Ovene married, but it was not until 1943 that they went to work in the bank—the same year their son Bobby was born.

In the 1950s, Ovene was in the middle of her life, a wife, mother and business woman, which was not unusual in the southwest where women, following in the tradition of the settlers' hard lives, worked along side their husbands. She did not attend college—at that time about the only college graduates in our town were the school teachers.

Her father Otha Osborn, who was called Othie, drove the school bus I rode from the time I started first grade until my family moved closer to town. He was large and stolid. I remember noticing his big shoulders as we drove to and from school. He was a man who smiled rarely, but I liked him and think he liked me. I'd heard some people say he had a temper, and I saw it one spring when the wind had drifted sand out of a field onto the dirt road. Now, my father said, the way you

155

get through a sand bed is to shift to first gear, then, slowly, patiently, careful to stay in the ruts, make your way to the other side. He shook his head at Othie's method, which was to stop several yards short of the bed, shift into low, and grip the steering wheel, one hand on each side. He would settle his large body even more firmly in the driver's seat and floor-board it. The forward momentum was supposed to jerk us to the other side. Morning and afternoon the five or six of us in the seats behind him pressed our own right feet against the floor until we felt the front wheels break free. But one after-noon the back wheels sank into the sand, and the harder he gunned the engine, the deeper they sank. Finally, he slammed the bus door open and pushed himself out to look at the tires. Somewhere in the front of the bus he found his shovel and said, "You have to get out." Some watched the shoveled sand spit into the air; others gazed across the fields and pastures.

The two generations of McFarlands were the core and the main support of the white wooden Baptist Church, located on the west edge of town, the only church in Logan that actu-ally looked like a real church, with its narrow Gothic style windows and small bell tower rising into the sky. I imagine the family there on a Sunday in the early Fifties, with one of those hard, cold eastern New Mexico March winds whipping up clouds of dust and sending tumble weeds careening down dirt roads. Inside the church, the floor is carpeted but a coal stove can't provide quite enough warmth for comfort. The McFarlands sit in their accustomed place on a wooden pew two or three rows from the pulpit. They attend almost without fail. If they miss, most of the congregation already knows why. The preacher keeps himself informed. Without their support, he knows he could soon be pastoring another small Baptist flock in some other, perhaps even smaller, hamlet.

Robert and Ovene's son Bobby, a big boy with a Humpty Dumpty body, thick brown hair parted on the side, and his father's eyes, sits between his parents. His mother and father are like two canyon walls on either side of him. It is warm between the two walls; it feels almost airless sometimes. He wants to doze but does not. While gusts of wind rattle the tall windows, he looks up at the preacher in his pulpit: the road to heaven is narrow, the way hard; only the baptized travel thereon.

Sometimes he is chosen as one of the boys who passes the collection plate. He takes this duty seriously, moving quietly from one aisle to the next and waiting for the round stainless steel collection plate with the circle of green felt in its bottom to mask the clink of dropping coins. It passes from hand to hand; when it returns to him he takes it carefully, for he has that desire so common to first or only children, the desire to be good and to please. He needs to please whenever he can, because he's not an especially good student and he has no athletic ability, that natural thing that in our small world could compensate for almost any other mediocrity. Already he knows others watch him and have expectations. Spontaneous behavior is suspect. Much depends upon his willingness to obey rules, accept admonitions, and hew to the narrow path.

By the middle of the 1950s, Bobby was a high school

freshman and I was a senior. My friend Jennie, a slender strawberry blond whose parents Lela and Harry Reid ran the local drugstore, was also a freshman, and I gathered that she and her friends considered him pretty much beneath notice. Besides being overweight and shy, he was "not too swift," she said, but he was nice, too, "not like Ovene."

I suspect he had few if any friends. He may have borne some of the brunt of the distaste Ovene aroused in some by her willingness to divide the world into those who were saved, those like herself, and those who were lost—namely any others. The two, large square people seemed to set themselves in judgment of the rest of us. In their view, sinners were easily recognizable, and anything was possible if you drank whiskey, smoked, played cards and danced. They were joined in this view by some members of the Church of Christ, who allowed no musical instruments in their church, and the Assembly of God, who were noted for their spirited church music and, some thought, unseemly religious fervor.

The unsaved consisted of the more liberal Methodists, some Democrats, some Republicans, and various smokers, drinkers, card players and dancers, along with those in the community who had no use for dogma of any kind. The Mexican population, about a third of the community living almost entirely on the south side of town, was both poor and Catholic, and therefore not allowed to speak authoritatively on any issue.

I accepted none of the strictures, but I liked the one against dancing least of all. I was not alone in this. A group of couples of my parent's generation sometimes called themselves dancing fools. Initially, Bob Rogers, a local farmer, made available a barn somewhere out in the country. I can still see the stream of headlights making their way through a pasture to the barn. Sometimes Doug Eastepp and brothers Jack Morper on guitar and Grant Morper on fiddle provided the music, but often it was a phonograph and records. Regulars like the Cain brothers, George and Miller Meeks, Ruth and Leaman Stewart, Fritz and Cliff Henderson (Cliff called the square dances), Harry and Lela Reid, Ben and Elsie Feerer and my parents, L. O. and Mable White, danced to tunes made famous by country stars like Red Foley, Eddy Arnold, Ernest Tubbs, and Hank Williams. The "Tennessee Waltz" always got played, and everybody had a good time with a PeeWee King tune:

> **. . . A man without a woman**
> **is like a ship without a sail,**
> **There's only one thing worse**
> **in the universe,**
> **and that's a woman without a man.**

Oh, ha, ha, said the women; oh, yeah, said the men.

Sometime in the late 1940s the American Legion got hold of a surplus army barracks to use as their Legion Hut, and eventually the group started holding Saturday night dances there. Roll Wright chose the records, trying to keep the dancers happy, and the younger generation took up dancing. Jackie McQuire, Bobby Bradshaw, son of Jewel Bradshaw and every local girl's heartthrob, Janet Love, Arelene Walker, Alvin Chance, (kindly brought to the dance by his uncle and aunt,

Tim and Mattie Chance) and me, danced many a mile.

The grown-ups kept their bottles of Jim Beam or Four Roses in their cars and small groups would leave the building now and again for a nip and visiting. I don't remember ever seeing anyone who had drunk too much; they had come for dancing and friendship. There was general disapproval of a married man who took a love struck interest in an embarrassed young widow, who strained away from him as he tried to hold her too close when they danced.

One Sunday morning after a dance the previous night, my parents and I drove into town to attend services at the Methodist Church. We whizzed by where the Legion Hut should have been, and I sat up straight and did a double take over my shoulder. There was nothing there. It had burned to the ground.

Some people thought that the fire had been set and said they knew who did it. "Aren't we going to get another one?" I asked my father. He didn't say yes or no. I never heard anybody say yes or no, but apparently nobody made a move to get another building. However, we younger ones didn't give up. We wanted dances in the school gym, especially junior and senior proms, but the school board, with Robert McFarland as its president, refused. Each year some incensed students protested the ban. After all it was "our" school. "They are so square," Jennie said, drawing a little square in the air with her forefinger.

We found other places. Often we turned to a woman named Mae Cobb, who had run the local bar after her husband died. She had moved the bar to a building on Highway 54 and let us use her empty building on Main street where the bar used to be.

Mae dyed the bit of hair she had dark red, and smoked. The bank deemed her and her saloon, with its cool, dim interior and old style, carved wooden bar than ran almost the length of the building, to be yet another den of iniquity and worked to close her bar down. She managed to hang on, and after the dust settled had a sign painted in big black letters over the entry to her bar: **WHISKEY THE ROAD TO RUIN.**

What did they think, Robert and Ovene, sitting upright and stolid in their four-door Buick, when they drove past Mae's mocking sign, her Chrysler parked beneath it? Perhaps they looked neither right nor left but straight ahead.

WHEN I LEFT LOGAN I WOULD have lost track of most of the lives there had I not married a boy, Eldon Walker, who had also grown up there. We kept up our connection through his sister Arelene Wright, a sociable woman whose life was filled with cooking for her family, coffees, Methodist church socials, and canasta parties. It was at the canasta table that she and Ovene became friends.

"Ovene?" I said. "*Canasta?* Has she taken up liquor, too?

"I don't think so," said Arelene, "but she's a pretty good card player."

Over the years I heard bits and pieces about the bankers and their son, usually after a holiday dinner when I joined others in Arelene's kitchen to wash and dry the dishes. There, dish towel in hand, I heard about Bobby's going away to the University of New Mexico in Albuquerque. Out from under his parents' supervision he sampled the unallowable. He drank and ran up gambling debts Robert paid off. Although the local people didn't consider drinking and gambling exactly constructive approaches to life, they thought of his behavior as just part of his growing up. It would stop eventually. He'd get it out of his system when the time came.

And he did. He married a young woman named Kathy Kelly, whose parents lived in Tucumcari, and he came home a married man.

THE BANK'S FOUNDER, SIM, known for years as The Old Man, was now truly old, his body thin and stooped. Robert and Ovene had bought the bank in 1962, retaining Sim as president. Along with banking, it was also now an insurance agency, and Ovene handled that part of the business. The prosperity of the times brought them perhaps more than they could have expected. Ovene now wore becoming clothes and had her hair done in a way that softened her heavy face. I saw her briefly one winter. Nothing softened what in her grey eyes seemed to me piercing and watchful.

Over time the after-dinner talk took on a different tone. In 1974 Bobby's young wife Kathy was pregnant again. The baby, a son, was born in January, 1975, the only son and fourth child born in five years. It was an unheard of number of children to be born with such rapidity into a white, Protestant, upstanding family. "People are saying don't they know how to stop that?" Arelene said.

The bank building that I remembered from childhood looked small from the outside but inside felt open and friendly. Sometime in the early 1970s I had business at the bank. I parked under the cottonwood tree, pushed open one of the wooden double doors and was confronted immediately with a high wall that curved three-quarters the length of the long room before meeting a floor-to-ceiling wall. In the long wall there were small openings set with iron bars. It looked like a bank in an old western movie. The teller told me the walls and bars were installed to discourage bank robbers, who reckoned the small bank easy prey. Still, it felt cramped.

"Yes, they are all crammed in there together," said Arelene. "There's too many of them there. I don't know how many people they think that bank can support." Ovene's brother and his wife had been brought into the business, and there were other employees in addition to Robert, Ovene, and Bobby. Somehow division developed. "I can tell you they hate one another," said Arelene, but she offered no details about who hated who.

"And Bobby is just not suited for it. He's always said he just wanted to be a cowboy. You know yourself you can't force somebody to be something they're not. Life's too short. They ought to just let him do what he wants to do—something he *can* do. He keeps saying he just wants to get out on a ranch somewhere."

"Don't fence me in," went a song popular a decade or so earlier: "Let me ride to the range where the West commences... can't stand hobbles and I can't stand fences, don't fence me in." There was a ranch for him to go to—the land Robert had returned to during the Depression. All the years I was growing up, Robert and Ovene lived in the white frame house on some of that land. From the highway travelers could see a side of the house, a windmill, and dead elm tree limbs twisting into the sky. In good times, the family stocked the land with registered Herefords, and in high school, Bobby, a 4-H member, showed his cattle at local fairs.

However, the ranch was sold in 1973. Instead of getting out on the ranch, Bobby was made president of the bank, and Robert became Chairman of the Board. Then one Christmas there was talk about the new houses the two families had built side by side on a hill in the north part of town, red brick for the parents, black brick for the son and his family, who'd moved into their new home over Thanksgiving of 1974.

Did the possibility of getting out on the ranch fade, along with the possibility of getting somewhere, *anywhere* away from the bank and the war there, where always, *always,* despite his title, he was the child and where he was slighted and his judgment questioned. *Somewhere* he and his family could be far from his parents' eyes and the townspeople's eyes, where he could be away from the questions about the children and how he and she were raising their children and why was he doing this—or that. Some far place where the care and discipline of the children would seem less formidable. Far from questions about the quarrels between him and her and far from her anger at him. *What was he? Did he have a life of his own, or what was he?*

And there was the state of the country, which sickened him: the Communists, Martin Luther King and the Negroes marching, the hippies and the war protestors, environmentalists, the new feminists, the black radicals, all of them bent on tearing the country apart.

Most townspeople despised the marchers, the hippies, and the war protesters. They felt betrayed. Those in rebellion among the white people were the college educated from prosperous homes, the ones for whom so much had been done and *was being* done, and they were not grateful. Instead, they shed their shoes, their shirts, their bras, and their American cleanliness. They attacked, and the attackees were stunned by the attack that began rudely and inexplicably. To them, the children came to seem like a swarm of grasshoppers that light in the pastures in August and shear off the grass at ground level. Perhaps they just had to be endured. But in time cities burned and screaming protesters threw rocks and revolutionaries blew up buildings and themselves, and Negroes became Black Panthers.

The townspeople considered the war protesters the most detestable of all. "What would Doc Thompson think?" they asked, referring to the old doctor's despair when his son Glenn was killed just weeks before the end of World War II. What of his boy's sacrifice? And the Mexican people, who laughed at the shoeless, shirtless, jiggling, draft-dodging, dirty Anglos. What of them? How could the Anglos keep their respect?

And what of the "environmentalists," who thought they

could tell people who had made a living off the land all their lives how to run their business. It was just more big government, and big government threatened and interfered in their lives.

During those years I was living in Portales, a town some hundred miles to the south. One Sunday I sat on my living room couch with my coffee and read the Letters to the Editor in the Albuquerque *Journal*. The letter that caught my eye was only one short paragraph. I don't remember any exact phrase, but through the years I've remembered its blast of rage. The writer — the son, husband, and father who just wanted to be a cowboy — hated protesters and especially hated environmentalists.

Some time later, on a Saturday morning in April, 1975, a month that in eastern New Mexico sometimes produces a late snow, more often a dry, hot wind, he went to the bank. Perhaps it was an errand or some unfinished chore, some last minute detail he had to attend to; perhaps it was to pick up a gun. Somebody said they saw him leave about ten. The day passed, and by late afternoon, his mother in her house realized she hadn't had any visits from the house next door, which, with the children always running back and forth, was unusual.

Ovene walked across her yard into theirs, knocked, and got no answer. She returned to her house, found a key, walked back, inserted the key and turned the knob of the door.

That's how it comes to me, her hand on a door knob, and I wonder if there was any notion at all, any sixth sense that what must have been long on the way had at last arrived. I think probably not. No expectation could match the reality. I want to say, "Stop. Listen a minute. Such silence. Don't go in. When you step inside, what you see will sweep away everything you've ever understood or believed or hoped for or thought you knew. Stand for a moment and listen to the afternoon."

THE SERVICES WERE HELD in the school gym that also served as an auditorium, the only place in town big enough to hold the six hundred chairs set up to accommodate the expected mourners. Spring leaves filled the tall elm trees in the school yard. The rose bushes that ran the length of the side of the gym nearest the school were ready to open their sweet smelling pink and yellow roses.

Inside the gym, a stunned gathering stared at the six caskets lined up in front of the stage. The Methodist preacher who would conduct the services had told an area newspaper that the community considered Bobby "a prince."

"Why did he do it?" people asked.

Murder-suicide cases in which a whole family is destroyed have been given the name familicide, or sometimes family annihilation. Although it makes headlines, familicide is very rare and as a consequence not studied in depth. It is also rare for a biological father to kill his children, but family annihilators are almost without exception fathers. Often the father kills himself, and that is his lone suicide note. In instances where the murderer survives, it appears that although there is rage and the rage is irrational, the murders are not spontaneous: they are methodical executions planned over a period of time. The father directs his rage at those he blames for his

167

problems. He kills his children to get even with his wife, whom he hates and blames, and to regain control of his life. That the murders are committed by a supposedly loving father is what makes them terrifying.

According to press reports, Bobby stabbed his wife and children. They were probably all dead before he shot each one at point blank range.

In 1984, Canadian anthropologist Elliott Leyton published *Compulsive Killers: The Story of Modern Multiple Murder."* His study is not about familicide, but about serial killers. While there are varied explanations for multiple murders, and while Leyton's book focuses on mass murderers who kill strangers instead of their families, his research into modern multiple murders may offer some insight into the McFarland case.

For Leyton, social systems present to individuals in the system "a matrix of choices and opportunities, rewards and punishments in terms of which each individual calculates his future." An individual in a given system considers "the roster" of available choices, and the choices he makes add up to or confirm an identity. Leyton thinks that the multiple murderer experiences at some point a kind of "internal social crises." The murderer concludes that he cannot get from the usual selections a life he considers worth living. The act of multiple murder becomes "a negotiated passage to a possible identity."

Why "negotiated"? And with whom is the killer negotiating? Not with any individual, but with his situation. The society says, "I can give you this, and this, and that," and the killer says, "I will take this because it gets me what I want."

What do such murderers want? One of the murderers Leyton considered was serial killer Edward Kemper, who lived in Santa Cruz, California, and conducted a series of murders that included the murder of his mother. Kemper had the intelligence to examine his motives, and Leyton quotes him as saying, " 'I'd feel inadequate there, feel like everybody's catching up with me, and I'm not doing anything.' " For Kemper, his murders became a "demonstration to the authorities," a way of letting the police and the community know "just how bad a foe they had come up against."

The reward is the demonstration to the authorities so powerful that they must consider it. It seems clear who "the authorities" in Bobby's life were: his mother and father, relatives, the various parts of the watching community, the government, God. Did Bobby have to accept the choices the society and its "authorities" offered? Perhaps he thought he did. Leyton describes serial killers as "profoundly conservative" because they accept whole heartedly the standards their society promulgates and admires. Although in fact they have many choices, none of which involves what Leyton calls "a massive refusal of life," such killers apparently lose—or never have—some sense of knowing what to do, how to solve a problem, how to fix things. Despite what they may consider their extraordinary effort, they cannot get what they want from life. The resulting frustration either pairs with or produces rage at those they consider responsible for their unbearable situation.

Leyton writes that his research indicates that multiple murderers do not "appear at random. . .but during periods of particular tension. Any crises in the larger system disorients the individuals in that system." The Sixties and Seventies must surely be counted as a period of "particular tension": the Cold War, assassinations, the Civil Rights movement, the Vietnam War, the youth rebellion, the feminist movement, and Watergate. As late as 1984 Leyton estimated that on average one American a month died as a result of mass murder.

Whatever misery time brings to the big world or the small, people carry on. In November of 1975 Robert and Ovene proposed to the congregation of the Baptist Church that a memorial fund be established to build an education building near the church in memory of the slain family. The 5700 square foot building was completed in September of 1977, the year Robert and Ovene sold the bank.

In his brief family history Robert remembered:

> **The family worked together at the bank, they enjoyed loading into the bronco 4-wheel drive pickup, going to the sandhill ranch to check cattle, fix windmills or wells. They were reluctant to give up the ranch because of the extra benefits of exercise and recreation. They loved the country where "the wind drew the water and the Cow chopped the wood."**
> **The sandhill ranch was sold in 1973.**

This bare mention of the sale of the ranch they loved opens up an area of conjecture. If they loved it, why did they sell it? How did they use the funds from the sale?

Robert wrote of Ovene that before they were married she liked to help him work cattle on the ranch, and after they were married he would joke that he married her "to keep from paying a cowpuncher $1.50 a day." She was, he wrote, "a top hand for 46 years." Strange as it may seem to some, this was probably the highest compliment he could have given. She died in 1980 of what Robert described as "a malignant condition."

In 1981 he married a widow who worked in the bank. He died in 1990, the last to go. They are buried in the Logan Cemetery not far from a bend in the Canadian River. The eight graves are all together, identified by small black marble headstones within a bed of dark red pebbles, all enclosed by a low black marble border. Of the children, Dawn Michelle was five, Vesper Anne, four, Cynthia Irene, one, Robert B., eleven weeks, their mother twenty-six.

WHEN AS A YOUNG WOMAN I left the town it was dying. I hold a "Last Picture Show" version of it, which is partly true but not the whole story. In the early 1960s the government built a dam on the Canadian River just west of town. Such a possibility had long been rumored, but townspeople had no expectations that any such government manna would actually fall on them. "I'll believe it when I see it," they said, and they saw it. Construction workers with paychecks, then recreation, tourists, boats, marinas, bait shops, and vacation and retirement houses built along the shore.

The town voted to tear down the old two-story sandstone school with its high curving windows, the only public building in town with the slightest distinction to it and the building that represented so much of the town's history. They razed it and replaced it with anonymous cinder blocks painted white. There are apparently few regrets. It was old, supporters of the change said, and dangerous. I was surprised at what a wrench I felt the first time I saw the squat, white building with its ordinary windows. For the first time, the range of life I'd seen within the old building's sandstone walls flashed upon me. Of course, all that "life" goes on within the cinderblock walls, and the community remodels and adds new buildings as the years go by.

When I was a girl, basketball games were what we did in the winter. As the population in the rural areas thinned, we sometimes had to drive several hours to find an opponent. We'd gather at the school, divide up in buses and cars and head out, full of talk and excitement. One night, two friends and I chose to ride back from a game with friends and had to wait a few minutes at the school for my parents to pick us up.

A storm had left a few inches of snow on the ground, then moved on. Now, near midnight, by the light of a full moon we could see the shadows the leafless elm branches cast on the trackless snow in the playground. Snow covered the wide concrete sidewalk and the half circle of steps leading up to the front door. It lay on the teeter-totters, on the iron bars of the small merry-go-round, and in wedges on the seats of the swings. It banked in the deep ledges of the windows. From the upstairs windows, like gods we high schoolers sometimes looked down at the children at play, sometimes saw them rush to meet a waiting mother. That night, in the silence of the late hour, the looming building, the shadows and the untrodden snow held a cold timelessness. We huddled together, glad when we saw the headlights of my parent's car come around the corner and we could get in and feel the heater's warmth.

We dropped off my friends and headed across the river to our house. When we got home, we'd do the routine chores. I'd brush my hair and get into my pajamas, my mother would dip her fingers into the jar of Pond's cold cream and lift her face to the mirror. My father would sit at the kitchen table and smoke his last cigarette of the day, looking out at the snowy pasture. Then, strangely confident, we would click off the lights and fall toward tomorrow.

Killing the Snake

The rough, arid farm and ranch country of eastern New Mexico where my father and mother, L. O. and Mable White, spent a good part of their lives is characterized by dry gullies, long horizons, and a silence that makes you feel like only the wind knows where you are. Every once in a while, a rattlesnake will sound its fierce warning: Don't tread on me. Although the people there might not know Emily Dickinson's poem, they know what it means to feel "Zero at the Bone."

The snake story is a staple of such places, and my father had his share. There was the hot afternoon he was horseback and stopped to rest and drink at a spring nestled among rocks and small cedars. The water created a shallow pond; he knelt, filled his cupped hands and brought the water to his mouth, then, half aware, made out the snake's body coiled in the water, its head resting on the surface not far from his own.

Then there was the time he and some neighbors were fixing fence on a sunny spring day, clearing a winter's worth of tumbleweeds off the barbed wire and away from the cedar posts. He scooped up an arm load of dry weeds caught at the base of a post only to find himself heart to heart with a

175

diamondback. "What did you do, L.O.?" someone would demand when he told that story.

"Got rid of it in a hell of a goddamned hurry," he'd say.

One morning in August when I was a girl of fourteen or fifteen, my father drove my mother and me in his aged Jeep out into the pasture to see how much water the previous night's rain had added to a dirt tank. I remember my father sitting down on some flat sandstone rocks that lay on top of the tank's dirt wall, lighting his cigarette and glancing to his right as he tossed away the match. Suddenly, he was on his feet, for he'd seen the snake, stretched out and sunning itself, a few feet from him.

He gathered up some rocks to kill it, for that's what people always did: they found a rock or got a hoe or a rifle and killed the snake. The battle was short but intense. Once the snake was under bombardment, its rattle electrified the morning. At one point it struck out powerfully, and my father had to jump back fast to avoid its bite. I remember him holding a big rock in both hands, raising it above his head and delivering the *coup de grace*.

We took the bumpy dirt road back to our house. I carried within me the noise and the sight of the brown earth and the bleached sky.

Some months later, a neighbor stopped by and in the course of his visit related how he'd killed a rattler down on the highway. Somehow this didn't suit my father. After the visitor left, he told my mother and me he'd decided to stop killing rattlesnakes. The thing that got him, he said, was they never got him, never even tried until they were in danger themselves and fighting for life, like the one at the tank, that was just there and quiet as anything and not a threat to anybody. They don't have a chance, he said, and besides, out in the pastures they keep down the rabbit and rodent population. So, he wasn't going to kill one unless it showed up on the back porch.

Maybe he was remembering the time when he and my mother first arrived in New Mexico and he got a job delivering government aid to people out on the prairie. He stopped at a dugout and on being asked to enter saw a rattlesnake curled up on the owner's bed.

"Hey, there's a snake on your bed!" he exclaimed. "Yeah," the old man said, "but don't worry. He's friendly."

Or, maybe he'd come to the time in his life when he no longer felt the need to impose himself on everything he surveyed, although he remained wilful, opinionated, and impatient. He liked the people he liked, and he liked a good story and good company.

He was the fifth son of a family of six boys and a girl. His sister Elizabeth White told me their mother said he was the smartest of the lot, and certainly I always thought he was the handsomest of them, six foot with greyish green eyes, an aquiline nose and good health and physique up to the time of his final illness. His family came by train to the hills of eastern Oklahoma in 1904S. They'd left their home near Charlotte, North Carolina, because his father ran through not only his own money but his wife's inheritance as well. Only the two older boys had enough where-with-all to become lawyers. In the prosperous Twenties my father sold Ford cars in Oklahoma and Arkansas; then, as it did so many others, the Great Depression drove him and my mother farther west.

They wound up in New Mexico probably because of a wiry Choctaw Indian they'd grown up with named Ike McLean, who was to my father and his older brother Earnest an adored part of their youth. When they talked about Ike, they gave their lives and his the flavor of a short story by O. Henry, a writer they admired. Ike, they said, was a charmer, and he charmed the deacons of a well known Baptist church in Oklahoma City until the stock market crash revealed a noticeable shortage in the accounts. He made it to the Oklahoma City airport just ahead of the deacons and the sheriff, showed a bush pilot some cash and said, "Take me as far as this will get me," which turned out not to be very far—a little town in the Texas Panhandle called Jayton—and from there he made his way into the big empty of eastern New Mexico.

Somehow my parents connected with Ike and with Granny McLean, who lived in a dugout somewhere out on the prairie. My parents homesteaded on some of the last homestead land in New Mexico and the U.S.—identified by area people as "across Ute Creek." This area west of Ute Creek was largely given over to tens of thousands of acres of ranch land, some of it part of the famous Bell Ranch. Ike and Granny lived somewhere in the vicinity, but eventually Ike moved on. My parents learned he was in California only when they received a photograph in the mail years later of Ike seated on a stool in an orange grove, one ankle propped on the other knee and his

Stetson set at a jaunty angle.

They endured the last years of the Dust Bowl, made some money during WWII and bought some land on the Logan side of Ute Creek. It seemed there was a chance life might become a settled thing until the drought of the Fifties hit when I was in the seventh or eighth grade. It was an anxious time; periodically my father broke out in hives or drank big glasses of buttermilk to quiet his ulcer. My parent's marriage, a struggle even in good times, became even more difficult as once again the land burned up, and all any creature could do was endure it.

My father was determined that I would go to college and sent me to the University of Oklahoma for a year though it stretched the family finances near the breaking point. I was glad to get away and certainly had no desire to accumulate my own snake lore, though I might sometimes tell one of my father's snake stories to amuse a city slicker. In fact, like many people, I have an irrational fear of snakes. When I was a kid, I got away fast if I saw or heard one, and I even hated the look of them in their glass boxes at the zoo.

Years passed, and then, the drought over and the pastures as lush as they can be in a dry country, I went back to the Plains with Eldon, my husband, and children Deanna and Bart (Waide had not yet arrived) to spend the summer where I'd grown up. One morning about six, I turned my head to look out the kitchen window just as I set my year-old son Bart in his high chair. I saw the serpent, head up, sedately snaking across the yard. Eldon was away for a few days with Deanna.

My parents had separated and my mother had been dead for several years; my father had moved into town. I was alone in the country with the baby, and I felt I couldn't let it go. I had no gun or rake, so I put the baby in his bed, went out and began—from some distance—to throw rocks at the snake, trying to chase it out of the yard. My plan was to run over it with the car.

I maneuvered the rattler out of the yard, half aware of our mutual terror. I got the car started, but I couldn't tell if I was running over it or not. When I backed away and got out to try to see it, I thought it was still under the car. Then I saw it slithering toward a nearby small mesquite and watched as the snake made one long, stretched out leap for the mesquite and what it hoped was safety. I moved the car close to the bush, got out and picked up a cedar post from a pile stacked against the yard fence.

I climbed on the hood of the car and began pounding where I thought it was. A fog of dust arose and I couldn't see much from the hood through the dust and the mesquite leaves and branches. Someone had told me that snakes keep twitching after they're really dead, but I didn't know for sure. Finally I quit, maneuvered my way off the hood of the car, and went back in the house, my brain filled with something like exploding short circuits.

I was standing at the kitchen window when I saw my father's car coming up the road. In the kitchen I told him what happened, and that I didn't know if I'd killed the snake or not. He went to look. When he came back in, he said, "That's the deadest snake I've ever seen."

I was in combat readiness for days, jumpy and wired. I couldn't keep my body from reacting; like the snake's; it kept on twitching. I wanted to forget it all, and I did. It was years before I told my snake story, and when I did tell it, I recalled the morning as a series of actions unaccompanied by any feeling.

More years went by before I thought about the snake itself, inching along in the green grass on that cloudless, crisp morning, probably headed for the water tank, and then, out of the blue, the bombardment. I remembered how the roar of the car's engine bounced back at me from the hard earth when I opened the door to see if I'd run over it. I remembered its long leap for survival.

My father and I never discussed the morning, but if it came up when others were around, something contemplative would appear on his face. Maybe he was surprised that I'd felt I had to kill it and that I'd been so afraid. He never indicated that he condemned what I'd done or approved of it, but I think it raised a question in his mind.

As for me, as the years have passed, I've thought about its meaning in my life from several angles. I've seen it as my personal experience with the fierce struggle that encompasses all of nature, and how in what's become my largely urban life, that struggle seems hardly to exist.

I've also thought about how mysterious the struggle is. One more snake story—the last one, I promise.

When I was a girl I used to walk in the pasture in the cool twilight. For a while, I had a little dog that went with me, a black and white shepherd mix who had appeared one day, as dogs sometimes did. On a walk, about a quarter mile from the house, we heard from its mesquite domain the snake's electrifying rattle. The dog barked and barked at it, but I persuaded her to come away, and we walked back to the house. As soon as we arrived, she turned around and, ignoring my call, took off running back down the road. A while later, she returned howling and snake bit. My mother beat two eggs in a saucer and set it out on the porch for her. She lapped them up without hesitation and lay down on her side, legs straight out in front of her, sick for several days, but after a while was up and about again. What imperative sent her back?

I've also looked at my encounter with the snake as saying something about fear and its opposite—security, or the perception of security. Although there must have been who knows how many rattlesnakes in the big mesquite bushes near the house, if I thought of that, I brushed it aside. After all, there was no way to eliminate the snake population. An intruder entered my yard domain and I eliminated it. Therefore, I watered my grass, tended to my red, orange, and yellow zinnias, and sat in my yard in the cool evenings.

How secure was I really? And my family? Who knows? It was one of those times when reality is a shifting thing, and what counts is how threatened—or how secure—we think we are.